London Borough
of Hounslow

Hounslow Library Services

This item should be returned or renewed by the latest date shown. If it is not required by another reader, you may renew it in person or by telephone (twice only). Please quote your library card number. A charge will be made for items returned or renewed after the date due.

My Family and Other Scousers

A LIVERPOOL BOY'S SUMMER OF ADVENTURE IN '69

DAVE JOY

The
History
Press

*For my family, then and now, but especially for
Victoria, Anthony and Heather to read to their
children and their children's children and keep
alive the memory of their 'Papa', Eric Joy.*

First published 2014

The History Press
The Mill, Brimscombe Port
Stroud, Gloucestershire, GL5 2QG
www.thehistorypress.co.uk

British Library Cataloguing in Publication Data.
A catalogue record for this book is available from the British Library.

ISBN 978 0 7509 5640 6

Typesetting and origination by The History Press
Printed in Great Britain

CONTENTS

ACKNOWLEDGEMENTS

There are a number of people who have contributed to this book being brought to fruition and I should like to thank them here:

Mum, Christine, Barry, Diane and Mark for their consent, trust and assistance; Chris Ford, my creative writing tutor, for his encouragement to begin this project; Rob Atherton, the older brother I never had, for invaluable feedback on early drafts; Doris Sumner and Inez Ashworth, the Golden Girls, for laughing their way through the final draft; Rita, for taking the time to read my manuscript and for her kind words; to the team at The History Press, for giving me the opportunity; and last but not least, Jean, the girl from the launderette who became my wife and best friend, for her unwavering love, support and patience.

FOREWORD

My Family and Other Scousers has such charm and innocence. It tells of a young boy's summer of adventure, when children had the freedom to play outside and use their imagination, taking them on great daredevil adventures where nothing was impossible.

We see how important family is, and how much they support and love each other. Young Deejay spends precious time with his beloved father on his milk round and revels in his family's great affinity with their working horses.

We are taken on wonderful journeys through the district of Garston, described with such clarity and affection that, as a reader, you are transported there too. Being from Garston myself, it brought back many childhood memories for me.

My Family and Other Scousers is a pleasure to read, and you will feel privileged to have spent the summer of 1969 with the Joy family.

Rita Tushingham, 2014

PROLOGUE

'You're a dirty old man, Eck Joy,' said me mum.
'I'm not old!' laughed me dad.
Some things never change.

The end of the 1960s was an exciting time to be an eleven-year-old. Liverpool born and bred, I had lived through a decade of social change, technological advancement and human achievement. Gone were the days of austerity and hardship that my mother would complain about every time she lectured us kids that we had never had it so good. On the cusp of what we expected to be an even more exciting decade, my friends and I looked to the future with huge doses of youthful optimism.

We already had first-class stamps on our letters and decimal coins in our pockets; 'the pill' was available on prescription; Francis Chichester had sailed – single handed – around the world; the first human heart had been transplanted; a few of us had colour television; and, of course, we all had the World

Cup – and *Thunderbirds*. If you lived in Liverpool you were particularly proud, because us Scousers had the Beatles and Cilla Black and Rita Tushingham. Now, jumbo jets were set to fill the skies, Concorde was ready to fly faster than the speed of sound and, most exciting of all, Apollo 11 was speeding its way to the Rocky Raccoon, one step away from winning the space race.

Despite all of this, and even though the swinging changes of the Sixties really were 'fab', it was nice to know that some things, good things, did not change. From my earliest memory, Mum had always scolded Dad for being old in some way or another: a dirty old man, a miserable old bugger or a silly old fool. Dad always laughed when he gave his ritual denial. His laugh was reassuring. It meant that everything was okay – F.A.B. It meant that there was nothing going on in the world that we could not cope with, nothing bad enough to stop the laughter.

Chapter One

ONE SMALL STEP …

Dad had just walked out of the dock office after seeing someone 'on business'. Lately, he had been seeing a lot of people 'on business'. When adults used that phrase I knew it meant: 'none of your business'. Nevertheless, I stood below the office window trying to earwig what was being said. I heard Dad laughing, but that was nothing out of the ordinary. Most of what I heard was just mumbling, though I had made out the word 'cheque' being used repeatedly. I presumed that this was something to do with paying for the sawdust.

He called 'thank you' to the half a dozen dock workers who had just helped carry the huge sacks of sawdust from the quayside saw mill and loaded them into the back of the milk van. They did not need to help; we could have managed by ourselves. They came out to look at the horse.

Now that my earwigging was done, I raced Dad back to the van, climbed in and sat myself on top of the sawdust sacks like 'the King of the Castle'. I breathed in the warm scent of freshly cut timber. With two clicks of his tongue and a shake of the reins, Uncle George urged Danny to walk on.

Danny was the oldest of our three horses and he no longer did the milk rounds as often as Rupert and Peggy. It was a long haul up Dock Road and it was best for him to take his time. And time was something I felt we had in abundance: this was the first weekend of the six weeks that would make up the school summer holidays. Dad and I had risen at six o'clock and then cycled down Chapel Road to the dairy — him on the road and me on the pavement. We had done the bottom round with Rupert and the top round with Peggy. Then, Dad and Uncle George had decided to squeeze in a sawdust run before lunch and take the opportunity to give Danny a bit of exercise.

I had done the rounds and the sawdust run on many occasions before, either at weekends or during school holidays. They were regular events for me, for my older sister, Ann, and for my younger brother, Billy. But this summer was going to be different. This was going to be the summer for which I had waited years. In the past, Ann had slept over at the dairy and spent whole days working with Dad. When I had asked for the same privilege I was told 'You're too young; you can when you're older'. That became Mum and Dad's stock answer, but I would not let the matter rest. Then, after what must have been two years of moithering, I applied a dose of logic to my argument. I pointed out that it was at the age of eleven that Ann was allowed to stay at the dairy. That was it, I had them – I could not possibly be too young any more.

Even so, it had taken them yonks to come to a decision. I could not understand why. Mum and Dad seemed to spend a ridiculous amount of time discussing it and what was more, they would go into the front room to discuss it; we only used the front room at Christmas or when we had guests. If I walked in, they would immediately cease their conversation, so I knew they were talking about it. Why the big debate? This was not exactly a life-changing event and quite frankly I thought it was taking favouritism a bit too far. But finally, my request was acceded to and arrangements were put in place for the coming summer: I would accompany Dad to work whenever I liked (within reason) and in the middle of the holidays I would sleep over at the dairy. This was my first day working at the dairy. One day I would do this for a living, but for now this was one small step in that direction.

I took great delight in being there, working with the horses and spending time with the adults, especially with my dad. He was one of those people who had been vaccinated with a gramophone needle – he loved to talk and I loved to listen. He seemed to know so much and seemed to take pride in letting you know how much he knew. Mum called him the 'Encyclopedia Eck-tannica' – 'full of useless information', she said. I did not think it was useless, though – I thought it was fascinating, even though I had heard most of his stories many times before. I was already well practiced at getting him started. I just had to ask him a question. It was like switching on the radiogram, generating a constant stream of verbal information. On this particular morning, these question-and-answer exchanges between the two of us made up for Uncle George's usual abstinence from conversation. Dad described

Uncle George as being 'a backbencher', which meant he did not say much. He would say just enough to communicate his meaning – no more and no less. For most of the time, this consisted of the word 'Aye'. But somehow, Uncle George was able to make that one word mean different things, depending on the context: an affirmation, a question, a complaint, a criticism, a request, a lament – even an expletive!

The dockworkers stood in a line, watching as we began the long walk back up Dock Road. There were six of them and they looked like the Trumpton Fire Brigade. The jingle 'Pugh! Pugh! Barney McGrew! Cuthbert! Dibble! Grubb!' popped into my head. It nearly popped out of my mouth, but I bit it back – I was too old now for that sort of stuff. From my throne of sacks I could see them through the open sides of the covered van and they were all smiling. There was something about a working horse that made people smile.

'Gerroff an' milk it!' shouted the youngest of the group.

'Ah! There's a wit and a half!' Dad called in reply as he stood in the doorway of the van and waved to acknowledge the would-be comedian. 'Or maybe just a half-wit,' he chuckled to us. 'Hell! You'd think they'd never seen a ruddy horse.'

'Aye,' agreed Uncle George.

I knew what Dad meant by that. I had heard him talk about it many times before. He had told me how generations of selective breeding had given carters the perfect partner with which to ply their various trades and how, for 250 years, the working horses of Liverpool had carried this great port on their backs. At their peak there were 20,000 of them working the city streets. But, by the 1960s most had been displaced by the internal combustion engine (or 'infernal combustion engine', according to Uncle George). A horse working the streets had become a rare sight. Dad said that horses had helped man deliver the industrial revolution and it was quite appropriate that the nineteenth century had been christened 'The Age of the Horse'. He also said how quickly we of the twentieth century had forgotten that debt.

'Did we have to pay for it?' I asked, referring to the sawdust.

'No, we get it Freeman, Hardy & Willis,' replied Dad. 'It's just waste to the saw mill people, a by-product that they can't use. In fact, it would cost them money to have it taken away. So they're happy for it to be taken for nowt and we're happy to take it for nowt. That way everyone is happy. Besides, it's grand for soaking up horse pee. Once it's soaked, it's so easy to sweep up and then put on the midden with the rest of the horse muck.' He laughed when he said the word 'pee' and so did I. 'Just think,' he went on, 'timber comes into this port from all over the world just for Danny, Rupert and Peggy to pee on it!' We both laughed again.

Uncle George gave two loud sneezes. He tucked the reins under his arm and pulled a dirty rag of a handkerchief out of his pocket. He blew hard and his catarrh sounded as thick as the oil slick on the Cast Iron Shore.

'Hell's bells,' laughed Dad. 'They can send a man to the moon, but they can't find a cure for the common cold!'

'Aye,' observed Uncle George.

Danny walked on. The needs of your horse always take priority and Danny needed to pace himself. There was plenty of room for any docks traffic to pass us, so we were not holding anyone up, but we were travelling fast enough to overtake any pedestrians.

'Ay-yup,' called Dad. 'Here's your Uncle Sid.'

I looked out the left side of the van and could see the back of Uncle Sid. He was walking home, wearing a donkey jacket over his overalls and smoking a pipe. He operated the big crane next to North Dock.

'G-o-o-o-o-d morning Syd-e-ny,' Dad announced as we drew alongside.

'Mornin', Eck,' acknowledged Uncle Sid, without breaking stride.

'Mornin', Uncle Sid,' I called and waved to him. He smiled, cocked his head and winked at me as we passed him by.

'Must have caught the early tide to be going home now,' Dad suggested.

'Aye,' agreed Uncle George.

'He's not really me uncle, is he?' I said.

'No, he's my cousin,' replied Dad.

'Explain it to me aggen, how that works,' I pleaded.

'Oh, alright then,' he sighed with false reluctance, before enthusiastically rattling it off. 'My mother, your nana, was Ellen Savage before she married my dad, your granddad, Percy Joy. Nana had two sisters, Sarah and Annie, and one brother, Sam. Sam Savage married Alice Whiteside and they had seven children: Doris, Stanley, Joseph, George, Margaret, Gordon and Sydney. That makes Sydney my cousin.'

I found family trees so confusing but Dad was able to recite them by heart – every root and branch, going back for gen-erations. He could even provide you with dates of births and deaths. I was amazed at how he kept it all in his head.

We trundled over the two unmanned railway crossings without sight of a train. Dock Road cut a beeline across the railway sidings that served the dockland. We referred to the land between the high street and the docks as 'the goods yards' or 'the goodsies'. The railway sidings branched across this piece of land like the veins of a leaf, moving goods in and out, connecting Garston Docks to the trunk of the country. According to the Encyclopedia Eck-tannica, there were ninety-three miles of railway sidings serving the docks.

Danny walked on. The last level crossing, at the top of Dock Road, was a manned crossing. As we approached it the signalman came down from the signal box and pulled the big white gates across the road. Uncle George pulled up Danny just short of the gates. After a minute or two the trucks appeared. They were all carrying a load of stone chippings, or 'Irish confetti' as it was known. There was a fairly long train of them, being shunted from the rear by one of the new diesels. They were very noisy as they clattered over the crossing. Danny stood as still as a statue.

'Don't the trucks frighten him, even just a bit?' I said.

'No,' replied Dad, 'he's a true Irish Vanner and a good'un at that.'

'Aye,' confirmed Uncle George.

Danny, Rupert and Peggy were all Irish Vanners. The term 'Vanner' referred to a breed of horse created specifically to pull gypsy caravans or tradesmen's wagons. Characteristically, they were strong and mobile and could maintain a steady, economical gait for hours at a time; they were intelligent and took instruction very easily with quick response; they could live on limited grazing and had a calm temperament; they were uniform in colour but with the occasional white face marking and had a good feather of hair on each leg. Danny was a bay, Rupert a chestnut and Peggy a black. All three had white face blazes.

The signalman put his hand up to us to indicate that there was another train coming. We waited. This time the diesel was at the front, pulling timber trucks, loaded with white, cut planks and beams. I so preferred the steam engines with their clock-face front ends, their great wheels, their rods and pistons and their smell of coal and steam. They had so much character, like the engines in the hand-sized 'Railway Series' books I used to borrow from Garston Library – but I was too old now for that sort of stuff. Over the last couple of years we had said a sad farewell to the impressive steam locos, as one by one they had been replaced by the impersonal diesels whose only feature of note was their wasp-striped rear ends.

'No more puffin' billies then,' I sighed.

'No. And it'll all be changing again with this containerisation idea,' warned Dad.

'Aye,' lamented Uncle George.

'What's containerizashun?' I said.

'It's the transportation of all goods in large steel containers, which can be put onto ships or can be loaded onto trains or lorries,' replied Dad. 'it will probably mean the end of lots of stevedore jobs on the docks.'

'Who's 'Stevie Door'?'

'Not 'Stevie Door',' laughed Dad. 'Stevedores. The men who load and unload the ships.'

'Oh. Does that mean Uncle Sid?'

'I don't think so,' Dad mused. 'They will probably still need cranes to load and unload the containers from the ships.'

He blew out his cheeks and then announced 'All change!' in mimicry of a platform conductor.

'Aye,' mourned Uncle George.

The signalman opened the gates and waved us on. He stood and admired the sight as Danny pulled us over the crossing and up towards the traffic lights at the top of the village. The lights changed to green as we reached them. The oncoming traffic passed us and Uncle George gave two clicks and a slap of the reins. Danny broke into a trot as Uncle George pulled him round to turn right onto St Mary's Road and into the hubbub of the village.

Chapter Two

WELLINGTON DAIRY

Garston village was always an anthill of shopping activity. It sat on a slope running approximately east to west. The busy high street, St Mary's Road, ran from the top to the bottom of the slope and was the backbone of the village. St Mary's Road was not a wide road, just a single carriageway, but it carried the load of a busy dockland as well as being part of the main riverside route into the south of the city of Liverpool. Huge lorries and No. 500 double-decker buses thundered up and down the village just a few feet away from the busy shoppers who crowded the narrow pavements on either side of the high street.

Uncle George kept Danny at a trot so that we would not hold up the village traffic. The pavements on both sides of the village were heaving; it was a Saturday and so the usual footfall of daily shoppers was swelled by those who worked weekdays. Plus, it was the beginning of the summer holidays. There was an expectant excitement in the air, a bit like the countdown of shopping days before Christmas – but without the snow.

The clop of Danny's metal-shod hooves cut through the clamour of pedestrians and vehicles and rang out to announce our coming. It was always the same when we trotted down the village: people would look up, heads would turn and faces would smile. It was as if we rode along creating a bow wave of cheer that broke over folk as we passed by. Some would acknowledge us with a nod or a wave. Dad seemed to know everyone.

'Mornin' Tom.'

''Ow do Betty.'

'Ay-up Bill.'

'Aye-aye Tubs.'

Then, as we approached the zebra crossing by Moss Street, he spotted Mum weaving her way through the sea of shoppers. He raised his cap and called, 'Good afternoon, Alice Joy!' Mum frowned and mouthed the words 'silly old fool'.

'I'm not old!' Dad laughed back.

Seeing Mum there brought back memories of my younger years, when she would 'take' me shopping. I used to be led through the shopping flotilla, held firmly by the wrist. This was to ensure that I did not get lost in the crowd or worse still, find my way under one of the thundering lorries. Mum had the knack of finding the rip tides within this flow of humanity and being able to quickly side-step and overtake. It was one of those survival skills she had acquired in her adolescence and had honed through years of practice. It was a skill that I was soon to acquire, but at that time I would merely bounce around in her wake like a rubber dinghy being towed behind a speedboat. For every one step she took I would fit in three or four. I was too small to see above the waves of pedestrians, so I had no sight of where we were heading. I would just focus on Mum's back and concentrate on keeping my feet moving under me. Thankfully, I was too old now for that sort of stuff.

Uncle George had Danny pull up at the 'zebra' and in a couple of strides Mum caught up with us.

'Can we give you a lift, Al?' Dad asked her. She thought about it with pursed lips.

'Yeah, come on Mum, gerron board,' I enthused.

'"Gerron"? It's "get on,"' she corrected me and then conceded to Dad, 'Oh, go on then,' as if she was doing us a favour. She checked the traffic and then stepped off the kerb.

'Give us a second, George,' said Dad.

'Aye,' confirmed Uncle George.

Dad gave her his hand. 'Allez-up!' he said as he pulled her up. Mum groaned with the strain of it. 'Welcome aboard, madam,' he mocked.

'Oh, thank you kindly, sir,' Mum reciprocated. She had an embarrassed smirk on her face as she sat down at the front of the van. This was great. I had never before seen Mum in the van. 'The last time I did this was before you were born,' she said to me. 'That was the week Dad had scarlet fever and I did the rounds with Uncle George, didn't I, George?'

'Aye,' replied Uncle George, before giving two clicks to get us underway once more.

Mum smirked at Uncle George's typically limited conversation and Dad and I just beamed at her, knowingly. Dad commented on how busy the village was today and Mum agreed. 'I've been to all three butchers and they've all sold out of Cumberland sausage. So, we're having Finnyaddy for tea.'

We looked out at the busy street scene as it scrolled past the sides of the van. The high street's two parallel facades of shoebox-sized shop fronts were interrupted by side streets. At these street corners stood a pub or bank or other larger store. The side streets to the west were all short cul-de-sacs truncated by the railway and docklands. But to the east lay a gridiron matrix of streets, all interconnected by entries and alleyways, or 'jiggers' as we called them. Most of the properties in the side streets were terraced houses, but randomly dropped in amongst these would be a small block of shops, a pub or a tradesman's yard.

We passed Heald Street with its police station, and then slowed to a walk to turn into Wellington Street. Dad stood at the nearside doorway of the van and gave a hand signal to indicate our intention to turn left. Wellington Street was one of those many side streets off St Mary's Road. It was connected in the gridiron to James Street, via Wood Street and Duke Street. We turned left into Wellington Street and then took a right into Duke Street.

On one side of the Duke Street/Wellington Street junction was a pub, unsurprisingly called 'The Duke of Wellington Hotel'. On the other side of the junction stood Wellington Dairy. There was a large sign on the building, which proudly announced in gold letters:

Wellington Dairy
A Joy & Sons
Farmers and Cowkeepers
Est. 1863

It was a family business run by my dad, my granddad and my great-uncle George. Dad referred to them as 'The Three Musketeers' – one day I would join them, like D'Artagnan! They all had farming in their blood and all possessed a love of working with horses. The family had its roots in the Yorkshire Dales and the elder family members still spoke with a Dales dialect. This influence had the effect of taking the edge off Dad's Scouse accent; he was a mixture of Scouser and Dalesman. In their labours the musketeers did not wear overalls or denims. They preferred the traditional three-piece workingman's suit (a 'three-piecer'). Their transportation was also traditional. None of the musketeers drove a car. The business was dependant on original horsepower.

'Oh, tell me aggen, Dad. Who was A. Joy?' I pleaded.

'"Aggen"? It's "Again",' stressed Mum.

'He was your great grandfather, Anthony Joy. I called him me "papa",' Dad began. 'His dad was Daniel Joy and his son was your granddad, Anthony Percival Joy; I'm Anthony Eric Joy and you're Anthony David Joy.'

'So "A. Joy" is like a family tradition, then?' I suggested.

'Aye. You could say that,' shrugged Dad.

'It's nothing to do with tradition,' interjected Mum. 'It was so that when a member of the family kicked the bucket, they wouldn't need to fork out to have the sign repainted.'

'Ah, shrewd businessmen, the Joys,' declared Dad.

'Aye,' snorted Uncle George.

'Shrewd businessmen, my eye,' argued Mum. 'A bunch of miserable old buggers, more like.'

'We're not old,' laughed Dad.

We pulled into the cobbled stable yard. They weren't actual 'cobbles' – according to the Encyclopedia Eck-tannica, they were 'stone-sets' – but everyone called them 'cobbles'. One end of the yard had two large gates that opened on to Duke Street and it had a number of outbuildings on the other three sides: the lean-to, the shippon, the water house, Danny's stable, the old stable and the brick midden. Rupert and Peggy were stabled in the shippon. Danny had his own stable.

The three horses were employed in pulling one of three vehicles. The first was the large four-wheeled covered van in which we had just been travelling. It was painted red and cream, once bright, now faded. There were no seats, just a raised box over the front axle. You drove it standing up with the reins coming through a window at the front of the van. It was kept in the yard. The second was a traditional two-wheeled open milk float, painted in black and gold with a single access between two seats at the rear. This was garaged in the lean-to. Next to the midden was stored the third vehicle: the four-wheeled muck wagon. Its sole purpose was for carrying, well, muck; that is, the contents of the midden, which was emptied about five times a year. The wagon had no seats. When it had a full load, Dad would just throw a blanket over the muck and sit on that. 'Where there's muck, there's money,' he would say. I had never ridden the muck wagon. As far as I was concerned, no amount of money was worth that.

Dad jumped down from the van, chocked a wheel and then helped Mum to alight. 'Are you coming in for a cuppa tea, Al?'

'No thank you,' she replied. 'I've not long had me elevenses and now I'm on my way to church to do the brasses.'

'Are you not even coming in to say "Hello"?'

'You're joking! What do they want to see me for?' she said, with an empty laugh. And then conceded: 'I'll see them when I get back.'

'Alright then,' said Dad.

'I'll see you later, chuck,' she called to me.

'F.A.B.' I replied.

She walked briskly out of the yard and turned out of sight down Duke Street. 'A lady in a hurry,' said Dad as we watched her go. We turned back towards the van to see that Uncle George had unhitched Danny and was examining the horse's left foreleg. 'Anything wrong, George?' Dad enquired.

'Aye,' declared Uncle George. 'A touch of lame. Heard it coming down the village.'

'Let's have a look at you then, me old fella-me-lad,' said Dad as he slapped Danny on his rump and then followed as Uncle George led the horse into the stable.

I was about to follow also, when there was a shout from the street and I turned to see six mischievous faces in the gateway to the yard; it was the Duke Street Kids. 'Deejay! Alright la!' called Tubs. 'Are you coming crocodile racing?'

Chapter Three

THE MAGNIFICENT SEVEN

Spending time at the dairy was not just about working with Dad. I also had a gang of friends who lived locally – 'the Duke Street Kids'. In the weekly comic *The Beano*, there was a strip about a gang of kids known as 'the Bash Street Kids'. They were quite a motley crew of extreme types. We did not consider ourselves to be quite as extreme or quite as motley, but we did like the idea of being in a gang that had an identity ('Join our mob and yer'll get ten bob!'). So, with a complete absence of imagination, we called ourselves 'The Duke Street Kids'. We were: Tubs, Shithead, Falco, Trebor and me, Deejay. We were all aged eleven and had just finished our last year at primary school. Our numbers were boosted by two honorary members: Uncle Robert and Bonzo, who were two years older than the rest of us (but, who had attended the same primary school). Seven in all – The Magnificent Seven!

Tubs was my bezzie mate. Because I had visited the dairy when I was younger, we knew each other even before we began primary school together. He lived over the betting shop on James Street and he had the biggest collection of badges you could ever have seen; because he had uncles in the forces, he had badges from all over the world. He kept them all in a big round biscuit tin. Due to the size of his ample waist, Tubs always seemed to wear pants that were too long for him. The rest of us had pants that came halfway down the thigh, but his came down to his knees. Even so, his pants were still tight around his full backside. We had a vague theory that there must have been a relationship between Tubs' weight, the tightness of his pants and the function of his digestive system because, more so than anyone else we knew, he was able to produce the most explosive, rip-snorting farts. He would usually give notice of an impending bodily erup-tion by quoting from Gerry Anderson: 'Thunderbirds are Go!' or 'Stand by for Action!' or even 'Anything could happen in the next half hour!' Then, once delivered, he would immediately burst into loud, goofy laughter that was totally contagious and would have us all rolling around tearful and breathless. When he wasn't laughing or farting, he tried very hard to be serious. He would hold his head high, purse his lips and stroke his chin as if he was doing some heavy think-ing. He thought it made him look important. We thought it made him look hilarious.

Trebor lived in Wood Street. He had never-combed mousy hair, freckles and knobbly knees. We called him Trebor because it sounded like his name, Trevor, and because of the advertising jingle, 'Trebor Mints are a minty bit strongerrrr ...' to which, with great invention he had added '... stick 'em up yer bum and they last a bit longerrrr!' When he sang that to us for the first time, we fell about – and the name stuck. He collected beer mats and had mounted them in an old photo album, from where they proclaimed such important messages as: 'A Double Diamond works wonders!' or 'Guinness is good for you!' or 'It looks good, tastes good, and by golly ...' Most of his beer mats came from his mum, who worked behind the bar at The Duke of Wellington. Rumour had it that Trebor's dad also spent time behind bars – but I don't think he ever brought any beer mats home with him.

Trebor was bezzie mates with Shithead, who lived in Wellington Street. Shithead was blonde – blonde hair, blonde eyebrows and blonde eyelashes. Shithead's real name was Brian. He was called 'Shithead' because his favourite word was 'shit' and because he collected, well, shit. Really! His collection consisted of a variety of animal droppings, each kept in a screw-capped jam jar and hidden in the outside lavvy at the bottom of his yard. Originally he had jars labelled as 'Rabbit', 'Guinea Pig', 'Dog', 'Cat' and of course, 'Horse'. But, after the circus had visited Garston Park, new jars had appeared labelled 'Zebra', 'Sea lion', 'Elephant', 'Tiger' and 'Camel'. Shithead swore to us all that these were genuine samples, but Falco said that all the jars should have been labelled 'Bull'.

Falco lived in Duke Street. He looked like Paul McCartney and all the girls fancied him. When he walked he bounced up and down like he had springs in his heels. He was called Falco because it was short for his surname: Falkland. He collected marbles and kept them in a drawstring cloth bag. He had hundreds of them: 'ollies', 'gobstoppers', 'steelies', 'stonies', 'creamies', 'aggies', 'bumblebees', 'cat's-eyes', 'tigers' and 'marmalisers'.

Falco lived next door to Uncle Robert, who really was Falco's uncle even though he was only two years older; Uncle Robert was Falco's mum's younger brother. Once we found this out we called him 'Uncle Robert' as a skit, but the name had stuck and we no longer thought anything of it. We all called him 'Uncle Robert'. He had crew-cut sandy brown hair and bandy legs. His pride and joy was his collection of picture cards from Brooke Bond tea. He had multiple albums full of sets of cards on every subject imaginable. He also had a couple of albums that his granddad had collected, but we weren't allowed to handle these because his mum said they were too valuable.

Uncle Robert was bezzie mates with Bonzo. Bonzo was big for his age. He had been the only kid to wear long pants before he left primary school. A mop of jet-black curly hair topped his broad smiling face and his thick eyebrows met above his nose like two hairy caterpillars in a head-on collision. He always wore the same red jumper, even in summer. He claimed that it was the only one that fitted him. The reason it still fitted him was because his nan would add more rows of knitting each time he grew a couple of inches taller. His passion was building Airfix model aircraft and he had dozens of them suspended by cotton from his bedroom ceiling, all frozen in a dogfight moment.

Whatever we did together, it inevitably turned into a competition of some sort or other. Who was the strongest or the toughest? Who could run the fastest or jump the furthest? Who could fart the loudest or pizz the highest? Bonzo was better than all of us at everything but he never bragged about it or imposed his will on us; he was a gentle giant. I could compete with the other lads at most things physical. I once had a school report that said I could 'run like the wind'. However, it was generally known that when it came to fighting, I couldn't punch a hole in a wet *Echo*. Whenever the possibility of a fight raised its head, I would get a severe case of butterflies. I reckoned they must have been cabbage whites – cowardy-custard cabbage whites. The nervous tension would shake in my knees and well up behind my eyes. I had developed three strategies when faced with the prospect of a fight. Strategy number one was to apologise and beg forgiveness; I found that people were less likely to hit you if you were pathetic. Strategy number two was to crack a joke; I found that people were less likely to hit you when they were laughing. Strategy number three was to run like the wind; I found that people were less likely to hit you when you were – somewhere else. These strategies did not make me feel any better; I still knew that I was a cowardy-custard cabbage white.

The Duke Street Kids always looked forward to my visits to the dairy because then we could all play in the stable yard and outbuildings. But we did not limit our activities to the business premises – the streets of Garston were just as much our playground. The best places for kids to play were the jiggers. They were virtually free of pedestrians and vehicles and provided a labyrinth of red-brick walls and quarried-stone flagging; sometimes following the slope and at other times following the level contours.

Our favourite game was 'crocodile racing'; it was our version of 'follow-my-leader'. Each of us Duke Street Kids would have a bike. The idea was to set off in a crocodile and for the leader to lose as many of the trailing pack as possible.

On a few occasions I had 'borrowed' Dad's milk bike from the stable yard lean-to. It was fitted front and rear with two angled-iron cradles; each designed to take a milk crate. It was a bike on an industrial scale. Although it seemed to weigh a ton, through secretive practising in the stable yard and shippon, I had learned to keep my balance on it – but only just. I was not quite tall enough to reach the pedals from the saddle, so I had to ride it standing up. I had christened it 'The Beast'! Why? Well, because it was a beast of a thing with a mind of its own, and once it gained momentum there followed a battle of wills between it and me as to what would happen next.

The seven of us would scream around the jiggers in the wild excitement of the chase. None of us had bikes with gears, so we would cycle uphill with innocent determination, recover along the flat, career downhill and then turn to assault the next slope. In the narrow jiggers we were inches away from the brick walls and oblivion. On our elbows, knuckles, shoulders and bare knees we all carried the scars and scabs of close encounters with catastrophe. Despite the danger, none of us had ever really come a cropper – though Tubs' elder sister had once come off while trying to ride down the church steps and she had broken a collarbone. Now that was a really stupid thing to do. The church steps comprised four flights down a stairway of solid sandstone rock. We called them the 'Death Steps' because adolescent legend had it that a drunk had gotten himself so kaylied one New Year's Eve that after midnight communion he had fallen down the steps, smashed his head open at the bottom and spilled his brains out onto the pavement – dead drunk!

When racing, we would hang on for dear life and scream all the way to the bottom of a sloping jigger before braking at the last possible moment and negotiating the next ninety-degree turn. Our cries would bounce off the stone walls and warn all of our approach. We each had our own signature. Tubs and me were both keen 'Fandersons' so he would sing the 'Thunderbirds March' and I, the theme tune from *Stingray*. Trebor would yodel Ron Ely Tarzan calls, Falco would cry 'Geronimo!' and Uncle Robert would do the 'Nee-na' mimic of *Z-Cars* police sirens. As for Shithead, well he would just shout 'Shiiiiiiiiit!' at every opportunity, and that would always make us laugh for some reason. Bonzo's used to be the theme tune from *Bonanza*, but since he left primary school he had dispensed with the need for a signature tune. Perhaps he thought he was too old now for that sort of stuff. If we encountered any unfortunate pedestrians they would flatten themselves against gateways and either cheer or curse as we flew past them like a blur of whooping Comanches in a John Wayne western.

We had no idea why our lungs would burn for breath, our bodies would shake and our legs would turn to jelly. In an adrenalin-induced euphoria we were oblivious to pain and exhaustion. Over the past couple of years we could tell that we were getting faster and faster and that the races were becoming more and more hazardous. We were growing; growing in stature, growing in strength, and growing in confidence.

So, now it was the first day of the school holidays and the lads were itching for another crocodile race.

'Can you get The Beast out?' Trebor called from the street.

'Yeah! Get The Beast out, Deejay,' echoed Falco.

'The Beast! The Beast! The Beast!' they began to chant.

'Alright! Alright!' I shushed. 'Hang on a mo.'

I went back to the stable and looked over the half door. Dad was busy examining the horse. I was sure he would not mind if I went out for a quick ride before lunch, especially as I had worked so hard all day. Nevertheless, when I pushed The Beast out of the lean-to, I did so as quietly as possible.

The lads had formed a crocodile in the jigger alongside the stable yard. I joined the back of it behind Tubs. From the front, Bonzo gave us a Cape Kennedy countdown from ten. When we reached 'blast off', Tubs stood up off his saddle, pointed his backside into the air and let rip with an explosive fart, which echoed in the confines of the jigger. We all burst out laughing but while everyone else managed to get going okay, I completely missed my footing and was left floundering behind. By the time I had remounted and put The Beast in motion they were already out of sight around the first corner and I was alone in the jigger. Approaching the ninety-degree turn I braked hard, and as I did so, someone stepped out from one of the rear gateways that opened out onto the jigger. It was 'Scally' Scales, the bully from the Catholic school.

Throughout my primary school years Scales had tried to catch me, but he had never succeeded; I could run like the wind. Now he had me trapped. He stepped in front of the bike and blocked my path. I came to a dead stop but I could not extricate myself from The Beast quick enough to make a run for it. As I staggered clear of the bike he tripped me up and pushed me to the ground, flat on my back. Before I could even attempt to get up he straddled me and sat down on top of my chest, pinning my arms above my head. He was two years older than me and he took full advantage of his greater size and strength. 'Got you at last, Joy,' he hissed through gritted teeth. He threw his head back and howled with delight.

As I struggled helplessly, he put his face close to mine and grinned down at me with his discoloured teeth and his eyes like black slits. My wasted exertions and his weight on my chest made me gasp for air and I inhaled his shitty breath. I felt like I was drowning in a midden. He leaned forward, pursed his lips and let a yocker of bubbly saliva build up and then begin to drop towards my face. He sucked it back in, laughed aloud and then began the torture again, savouring each moment.

I needed a way out, but none of my usual strategies were going to work here. The jigger we were in ran at the side of the stable yard; you could tell because the stable walls were made of thick sandstone blocks rather than the much thinner red brick that lined the rest of the jigger, enclosing the backyards of all the terraced properties. I thought about shouting for help but I realised that Dad and Uncle George were in Danny's stable and that the same sandstone would ensure my cries went unheard.

I looked up at that awful yocker yo-yoing above me. This time I knew he was going to let it fall, so I turned my head away and sealed my mouth. I could feel his body on top of me. He was shaking with suppressed laughter and eager anticipation. Then, suddenly, I could not feel him at all. I turned back and looked up to see him suspended above me with the now frothy yocker dribbling down his chin and on to his jumper. Bonzo was holding him by the scruff of his neck.

'Why don't you try picking on someone your own size, Scales?' Bonzo challenged as he threw him down the jigger like he was a broken *Watch with Mother* puppet. Scales slowly picked himself up and sneered at Bonzo. By then the rest of the Duke Street Kids had arrived in the jigger and I scrambled up to join them, the five younger members standing behind Bonzo and Uncle Robert. Not surprisingly, Scales decided to decline Bonzo's invitation. His sneer turned into a smarmy smile and he pointed at me. 'I'll get you, Joy,' he threatened.

'Pizzoff, Scales,' warned Bonzo. With that, Scales gave a mocking laugh and then turned to jog away down the jigger.

'You alright, Deejay?' Uncle Robert asked when Scales was gone.

'Yeah. He was going to spit on my face but you stopped him just in time. Thanks, Bonzo.'

Bonzo was back to his usual nonchalant self. 'That's okay, matey,' he shrugged.

'You should have hit him,' complained Falco.

'Nah. He's not worth it,' replied the gentle giant. 'Come 'ed, let's get racing.'

We reformed the crocodile but this time with Tubs in the lead and Bonzo bringing up the rear, behind me – just in case Scales reappeared. As we set off I could feel that cowardy-custard cabbage white feeling in my stomach and my legs were shaking as if I had already completed one gruelling race.

To everyone's surprise, Tubs set a cracking pace. He was a bit slow on the football pitch and I could always beat him; but on a bike his weight worked in his favour and those chubby legs pumped like pistons. He had never lost me in a crocodile race before but he seemed determined to do so this time.

After half an hour, Tubs' cracking pace was taking its toll and I for one was nearly goosed. Usually, I could more than hold my own in these races, but I was clearly out of sorts after my experience with Scales. Bonzo had already overtaken me and I was now bringing up the rear once again, this time behind Shithead. We raced down Wood Street, which was the only jigger with a proper name, and emerged opposite Garston Hospital. I caught sight of the end of the crocodile. They had crossed over Woolton Road and were making their way down to the bottom of the village. I had to stop and wait before crossing, as there was a No. 80 bus coming down Woolton Road. The bus passed me and I managed to get The Beast moving again, but the others were way ahead of me.

I crossed the road and bumped up onto the far pavement. I could see the tail-enders. They had dismounted and were pushing their bikes across the traffic lights. The riders at the front had already cleared the junction and were remounting. It was plain that I had a lot of ground to make up and it was looking like they were going to lose me. I poured my weight into each push of the pedals in order to increase my speed. As I approached the junction, the lights changed in my favour. I made a snap decision. A quick check over my shoulder and then I launched The Beast off the pavement. The No. 80 bus was just pulling away and I managed to fall in behind it. Using the momentum from the downhill slope, I rode in its shadow across the junction. When I reached the other side I bounced back onto the pavement. Shithead was just ahead of me – I had made up the ground and was nearly back in touch.

Tubs led the crocodile under the bridge and I could hear the lads' signature tunes echoing back to me. On the other side of the bridge was the church, and as we emerged, I caught a quick glimpse of someone beginning to come down the church steps – it was Mum! Hell's bells! I'd forgotten she was going to church to do the brasses. For a moment I wondered why she was coming out now, because doing the brasses usually took hours. But then the survival instinct took over – if she saw me cycling down here, she'd throw a wobbler. I rode as close to the church wall as possible to keep myself out of her line of vision and pushed The Beast to go as fast as it could in order to get me round the bend of Church Road before Mum reached the bottom of the steps. As I sped around the ninety-degree turn onto Banks Road, I glanced back to see Mum emerging from the gateway. Phew! I'd made it, unseen.

Once round the corner I expected to see the other riders ahead of me, but there was no sign of any of them. Then I realised – the lychgate! Shit! They had turned into the churchyard. None of the other lads were members of the church, so they weren't bothered about getting caught cycling around the churchyard, but I was in the choir – if I got caught, Mum would have me flogged in public! I was sure that Tubs had taken this route deliberately, thinking that I would be too scared to follow. I hesitated. I could just wait at the lychgate as they would eventually have to come back this way, but then they would say that I was a coward. I looked up the churchyard and could see that they were now cycling around the church. I decided to risk getting caught and do just one circuit of the church to prove I wasn't a coward – after all, I had just seen Mum leaving the premises.

The path from the lychgate was steep, so I braced my back against the point of the saddle to give myself better leverage in pushing down the pedals. The Beast lumbered its way up the incline. When I reached the church, I fell in behind Shithead and began to circle the building in a clockwise direction. I prayed that no one would come out and recognise me. I cycled past the main entrance at the top of the Death Steps, past the vestry door, alongside the railway and then past the gasworks. At each bend I would catch a glimpse of Shithead, just ahead of me. When I completed a circuit and looked back down the churchyard towards the lychgate, I could see no sign of the riders there – they must be doing another circuit. I decided to push my luck and go around one more time, but this would be my last circuit. After that I would free wheel back down the path to Banks Road and wait for them there.

I pushed The Beast onwards again, wary of any riders trying to lap me. This time when I came around the front of the church, I couldn't believe my eyes. I caught sight of Shithead as he turned down the steps. Surely this was a joke. It was stupidity to try to ride the Death Steps. But as I looked down upon Church Road, there was Tubs on the far side, sitting astride his bike, waiting. He had done it. They were all doing it – Hell's bells and buckets of blood!

Shithead's yell of 'Shiiiiiiiiiiiiii-', ended abruptly as he disappeared down the first flight. If I did not catch up with them now not only would I lose the race, but I would also be branded a coward. God, please let Mum be halfway up the village by now, I prayed. I focused on the point where Shithead had disappeared and I edged The Beast forward with sweat beginning to sting my eyes.

This – was – it.

I lined up The Beast in the centre and rolled toward the top step. As I approached, I could see across to the upstairs windows of the shops on the other side of Church Road – that's how high up I was. The thought of my brains being spilled on the pavement below flashed through my mind, then the front wheel dropped over the first step and there was no going back. The Beast bucked like a bronco. I suppressed a cry of fear. If I had been sitting on the saddle I'm sure I would have been pitched over the handlebars, but standing on the pedals with bent knees must have given me a low centre of gravity and the ability to absorb the shock of each impact. Bang-bang-bang-bang – down the first flight of four steps.

I'd cleared one flight and I was still riding – so, it was possible. But, when I hit the first of the flat landings the handlebars came up to smack me under the chin. The Beast must have sensed my weakness and momentarily, it took control. It bounced us both towards the left-hand wall. Hellfire! Clipping a wall in a jigger was one thing but clipping a wall on the Death Steps would be instant, well, death. The panic rose in my throat. I felt as though it would emerge as a roar but it came out as a desperate whimper. I pulled the handlebars with my left and pushed at them with my right, using every ounce of strength in my young arms. The angle of the front cradle hit the wall and ground a scar into the sandstone. Instinctively, I wrenched control from The Beast and together we cannoned off the wall, back towards the centre line. We pitched forward again as we hit the second set of steps and I fought to retain my balance. Bang-bang-bang-bang-bang! – down five more bone-shaking, jaw-juddering, solid stone steps. We repeated this twice more, each flight of steps bringing me nearer to the safety of flat ground. We cleared the last step. The rear wheel dropped and we were back on the level. I breathed again and tasted blood in my mouth. I hadn't realised I had been holding my breath. I hadn't realised that I had bitten my lip.

I'd done it! I'd ridden the Death Steps and I'd tamed The Beast – and I was still alive! Just as the adrenalin rush began to break over me I realised that I had one more manoeuvre to complete – I had to angle myself through the gateway and back onto Church Road. The thought of surviving the Death Steps only to be killed by a random lorry temporarily stemmed my jubilation. But the road was clear and there on the other side, sitting astride their bikes, were the other six riders, each with the same look of exhilaration that I must have been wearing. They were all laughing hyperactively and cheering, whilst at the same time fighting for breath. I rode over and joined them. Our sheer delight in a shared thrill spilled over in exuberant, gibbering exchanges of who had done what, accentuated by the occasional 'Fugginell!' from Uncle Robert, 'Berloody!' from Tubs or 'Shit!' from Shithead.

Eventually the adrenalin subsided and we began to get our breath back. I said I needed to get back to working with my dad. At my insistence we made our way back via the jiggers – I wanted to avoid being spotted by Mum. We entered the stable yard like returning astronauts, still beaming with the triumph of our death-defying achievement. As I pushed The Beast back under the lean-to, Dad came out of the shippon. He took in the scene of seven grinning riders and their bikes and then looked at me with a slight frown. I hadn't asked if I could use the bike.

'Where've you been?' he asked of me.

'Oh, just 'round the block,' I replied as casually as possible.

'Aye. Well, just be careful to stay off the roads, then,' he said, 'they're dangerous.'

'No need to worry about that, Dad,' I assured him. 'We always keep off the dangerous roads.'

Chapter Four

FAMILY MATTERS

The lads peddled off down Duke Street and left Dad and me alone in the yard. For a moment there was an uncomfortable silence. The excitement of the race was still gushing up inside me like a shaken bottle of cream soda, but I thought better of telling Dad just now; he might not approve. Instead, I filled the void with a tactful change of subject.

'How's Danny?' I said. But before Dad could answer, Mum appeared at the gateway and marched into the yard. I was half expecting a reprimand but she obviously hadn't seen me out cycling with the lads. Instead she announced in frustration that they had run out of Brasso, so she had not been able to do the brasses. There followed a quick discussion about whether I would have my lunch at the dairy and go home later with Dad, or go with Mum now and have something to eat at home. Dad said he had things to do; something about buying plates and seeing someone 'on business'. That sounded pretty boring to me, so I felt only the minimum of reluctance when they decided that I would accompany Mum, her walking and me on my bike.

We made our way into the dairy to say goodbye to Nana and Granddad. The business premises consisted of two properties. As well as the stable yard there was also No. 37 Wellington Street, where Nana and Granddad lived. It was an end terrace and there was a side entrance from Duke Street that was used by the public. This led to a covered yard with two outbuildings: the 'cold room' and the 'hot room'. In the old days the 'cold room' was where cheese, cream and butter had been made. It had a wide solid slate slab built into one wall, like a worktop, which was now used to store dairy products and keep them cool. If you put your hand on the cold slab you could feel it drawing the heat out of you. There was also an old kitchen chest of drawers in which Dad stored his tools for fixing the carts or repairing harnesses. The 'hot room' was hot because it had a glass roof reinforced with wire. Dad had told me that it hadn't always had a glass roof. When it was an air-raid shelter it had a thick concrete roof, but that had been taken away after the war was over. Now Granddad used it as a greenhouse and kept his tomato plants in there. Nana used it as a wash house. As well as a washing line, there was also a clothes mangle, a four-legged wooden dolly peg and a galvanised steel dolly tub. Together, they looked like instruments of torture from a Vincent Price movie. In the covered yard, milk for sale to the public was stacked in crates against the house wall to keep it as cool as possible. The house, yard and outbuildings were known collectively as 'the dairy'. All of the walls were whitewashed and the stone floor was always scrubbed spotlessly clean.

A passageway between the two outbuildings ran down past the outside toilet to the bottom of the yard where it emerged into the jigger, immediately opposite the doorway that led to the stable yard. The jigger was only narrow and I could just about jump from one property to the other without touching the jigger floor.

I ran up the passageway into the covered yard. Nana and Granddad's black cat, Arthur, was sitting at the bottom of the kitchen steps and he stretched up appreciatively as I gave him a quick scratch on the top of his head. I skipped up the steps to find Nana taking the whistling kettle off the electric stove and Granddad in the hallway, placing the telephone handset back in its cradle. Nana and Granddad were the only people I knew who had a phone. It was a heavy black Bakelite thing with a shiny chrome dial, but we kids were not allowed to touch it because it was only for use 'on business'. I explained that I was now going home with Mum; she stood in the covered yard and did not enter the house.

'Hello Alice,' said Granddad, coming to the top of the steps. Arthur ran into the house.

'Hello, Granddad. Hello, Nana,' she replied in her usual business-like fashion. She always called them that. It was never 'Percy and Ellen' or 'Mum and Dad', but always 'Nana and Granddad'. We three children used these terms affectionately, but it was not quite the same coming from Mum.

I retrieved my bike from the cold room and we set out for home. Home was two-one-eight Garston Old Road, a terraced house overlooking Garston Park. That is where I had lived all my life. It was great living opposite the park. But, it was also great visiting the dairy. So, my family lived this odd existence, with all of us regularly making the journey up and down Chapel Road.

I cycled steadily alongside Mum as we ascended the long slope up to the railway bridge. She had a lifetime of practice of walking everywhere in Garston, and now she was almost as economic on her feet as an Irish Vanner. I did most of the talking on the way home. I rattled on about everything I was planning to do this summer; this was going to be the best summer ever. Mum was not as talkative as Dad. In fact, they were complete opposites. 'Opposites attract,' they would say.

Mum came from a large family; she had nine brothers and one sister (Aunty Amy). She said that she had grown up as a tomboy, playing with her brothers. She also grew up living in the tennies, which is probably why she was a hard-knock. Mum had a habit of always saying what she thought. She once told Granddad that he was a dirty old man. He used to fart in front of us children and he would say, 'Did you hear a mouse squeak just then?' We thought that was hilarious. One day he did it in front of Mum; he never did it again after that. When Mum was not around I would ask him where the mouse was. He would laugh and whisper that Arthur had caught it. That became our secret joke. I liked having this secret with him. It made me feel special.

One thing that Mum and Dad did have in common was their involvement with the church, Garston parish church, St Michael's. They had met through the church's Youth Fellowship and of course, were married in the church. After that, Mum was in Young Wives, then Pram Club and then Mothers' Union. She also helped out by polishing the brasses and embroidering kneelers. Dad's job limited the time he had available, but he did help out with the maintenance of the graveyard. He did not work on a Sunday, so they both attended church, well, religiously. When we were younger we were made to go to Sunday school. We hated that – an hour and a half of reading the Children's Illustrated Bible, singing songs and saying prayers. Fortunately, we were too old now for that sort of stuff. Instead, Billy and I were in the choir and Ann was a bell ringer. We didn't hate that, though – you got paid for doing that.

Dad said he had married Mum because she had 'horse sense', and by that he meant that she wouldn't nag him. He also said that the differences between him and Mum complemented rather than conflicted with each other. He said that this was why they never really rowed. Although Mum was hot-headed and quick to come to the boil, Dad always kept his cool. If she would take off like a Saturn V rocket, he would be a Sea of Tranquillity. Consequently, their 'rows' would take one of three forms.

The first scenario was a simple discussion of the plusses and minuses, resulting in an agreed plan of action. In the second scenario Mum would see things one way and Dad another. This was the version Dad seemed to enjoy the most. He would energetically put across his point of view but as Mum came close to boiling point, he would read the signs and respond by playing the part of the subservient, hen-pecked husband, and with a roll of his eyes, he would concede and accommodate Mum's wishes. This version would typically end with Mum scolding him for being old and him laughing his denial.

Because Dad was so accommodating, the third scenario was a rare occurrence. In this version there wasn't any arguing and there wasn't any humour. Dad would firmly but quietly state his position without any show or ceremony. This would happen if, for example, there was a matter of principle at stake. Mum could read those signs and she knew no amount of heat on her part would make any difference, so she would quickly move the topic on to something else; on to something she knew she could win.

On our way up the hill we passed St Francis of Assisi Roman Catholic Primary School. One thing that I would not miss about leaving primary school was being chased by the Catholics. The left-footers always hunted in packs and would invariably come across you when you were alone or with just your brother or sister. They never caught me – I could run like the wind. When we were in the infants, we taunted each other. We called them a bunch of 'sissies', they called us 'proddy-dogs'. We did not know what that meant until we asked Mum; she never seemed to have much time for Catholics (Dad said they made her cross). She told us that 'proddy-dog' was slang for 'protestant', but we were none the wiser. She said that they must teach them rubbish at that school, because we were not protestant at all, we were Church of England. Next time they taunted us we told them that they must be taught rubbish at that school, because we weren't protestant at all, we were Church of England – then we legged it.

For the most part this was all harmless - just name-calling and chasing. But then there was Scally Scales, the bully from earlier. He lived in James Street with his family of scallies. There always seemed to be at least one member of his family in jail. We used to sing 'All the Scales – live in jails!' but I was too old now for that sort of stuff. Whenever you heard adults mention him, they shook their heads when they said his name. When Scales caught a proddy-dog, he thumped them, or worse. There was nothing nice about Scales; even the other Catholics avoided him.

We broached the top of the hill, passed over the bridge and on to the five-star junction where Chapel Road met with Garston Old Road, Island Road, Bowden Road and Seddon Road. Standing tall on this junction was our school: St Mary's Church of England Primary School. Not only was this the same school Dad had attended, but all three of us attended it as well; Billy was still there and Ann had been top of the class. My favourite teacher had been Mrs Paisley. Her husband was the trainer at Liverpool Football Club. I supported Everton ('Tony Hateley isn't worth a ha'penny!') – but she was still my favourite teacher. She had taught me multiplication. 'Mrs Joy,' she had announced, 'the penny has finally dropped!' It had taken me ages to understand multiplication; Ann had got it first time. Mum said I had inherited my running from her because she had been a tomboy, but that Ann had inherited her multiplication from Dad – he didn't need to use a paper and pen as he could work everything out in his head.

We crossed the arms of the junction. On the corner of Bowden Road and Garston Old Road there was a small triangular island of land fronting a short row of shops. The island was home to a number of tall sycamore trees and was surrounded by a low privet hedge, broken in many places where the kids had created short cuts.

Mum could have done all of her shopping in the village or at Garston Market, but she liked to use the local shops as much as possible. She said that if we didn't use them, they'd go out of business. The shops at the top end of Garston Old Road included Winney Inch's wool shop and hairdressers and also Tushingham's grocers and post office. We were all really proud to be able to shop at 'Tushies' as Rita Tushingham was a famous movie star – almost as famous as the Beatles. The row of shops at this, the bottom end of Garston Old Road, included the 'Laundermat' launderette and drycleaners, Banks' grocery and Jennings' newsagent.

Mum went in to Banks' to buy some boiled ham. Mr Banks was a grocer but not a greengrocer. For fruit and vegetables we depended on Tommy Stevenson and his mobile shop. He came around once a week and spent the morning parked right outside our house. Mums from all over the block visited his wagon for their weekly greens. They would then stand around on the pavement, gossiping for ages; it was a social occasion. Some mums came by car and would load up their boots with bags of fresh produce. There was one car I looked out for. It always had a load of kids in the back, including a girl who I had seen working in the launderette. When she saw me, she always smiled. When she smiled at me, something happened and I always smiled back. I had no choice – I couldn't help myself. I never told anyone about the girl in the launderette.

While Mum was shopping in Banks', I cycled clockwise around the island, like an orbiting spacecraft. Each time I passed the launderette I slowed down and peered through the big, long windows of what was actually two shops knocked into one. On my third pass I saw her. I watched her over my left shoulder as I passed the windows. She looked up from what she was doing and saw me. She smiled. I smiled back. I held her gaze until I passed beyond the window. There was a tingling on the back of my neck that flowed up behind my ears and reached the top of my head. I enjoyed that feeling. It came with a warm glow.

I turned to face front and there, dead ahead, was Miss Spinner, with a shopping bag in each hand. As I bore down on her, I swerved to my left to avoid a collision, but she sidestepped to her right. As I turned to my right to avoid her, she sidestepped to her left to avoid me. It was like some sort of slow-motion comic dance, except it was about to end in calamity. An instant before I mowed her down, I hit the brakes. As I did so, I slid from my seat to get my feet on the ground but the jar of the brakes made me miss my footing. The crossbar caught me right between the legs. Berloody 'ell! A crossbar in the Niagara Falls is the most embarrassing and numbing sort of pain a lad can experience. Dad said it could ruin your wedding. I didn't know about that (why would anyone get married on a bike anyway?), but it did knock the breath out of me. I looked into the eighty-year-old spinster's eyes for a hint of understanding or sympathy, but found neither.

'Shouldn't be cycling on the pavement,' she scolded.

'Sorry, Mizz Spinner,' I managed, between clenched teeth.

She sidestepped once more and passed me by. I dismounted and pushed the bike away from the launderette, hoping no one in there had seen what had happened. I waited outside Banks' and caught my breath. The pain in my groin began to subside but the warm glow in my chest and head persisted. It was a new and intriguing feeling, something I had never experienced until I looked at the girl from the launderette. Before then, girls had just been, well, girls. And, of course, all boys hated girls. They came in two varieties: younger sisters and older sisters. Boys hated older sisters because they were so bossy and boys hated younger sisters because they were so inconvenient. And, as every girl reminded us of our sisters, boys treated all girls the same; that was just the way it was, like a natural law. At least, that was the way it had always been, but now I was not so sure.

Mum emerged from the grocers. The pain had gone but I decided I'd walk the rest of the way home, just to be on the safe side. As we turned the corner to face Garston Park, I became aware of the hullaballoo of young voices from the playground across the road. Although it was late afternoon, the playground was still teeming with kids, all celebrating the beginning of the summer holidays. This was the only playground for miles around and so all of the kids in the area converged here, bringing pennies with them to spend at Jennings' newsagent. There was a feeding trail of discarded wrappers between the playground and the shop. As Mum and I passed through the litter field, I kept a watchful eye out for Fab wrappers. It was meant to be a girl's ice lolly, but the wrappers now included 'On Safari' cards. I was fascinated with wildlife and I already had the wall chart pinned up in my bedroom. Whenever I bought one I would always ask 'Can I have a Fab lolly for me sister, please?' to make it quite clear to everyone that I was not buying a girl's lolly for myself. Most of my collection, though, came from discarded wrappers. Mum tolerated me picking up litter off the floor or out of the litter bins for this one purpose only, but she insisted I washed my hands as soon as I got home. There were forty cards in all and I only needed one more to complete the wall chart: card number eight, the leopard.

We walked on along Garston Old Road, crossing the side streets. Inspired by the Encyclopedia Eck-tannica, I had memorised the running order of the streets: Ebrington, Basing, Bellmore, Belper, Calthorpe, Lumley, Stormont, and Whithedge. I knew at least one person in each street. Dad seemed to know everyone in every street here, as this was his top round. We lived between Bellmore and Belper, overlooking the park. Everyone called it Garston Park. Everyone, that is, except 'the Corpy', or Liverpool Corporation; they called it 'Long Lane Recreation Ground'. Somehow, the name Garston Park sounded much nicer, much warmer, more personal. In fact, the park was very personal to the Joy family. Dad said that the park was created in 1901, but that before then it had been three fields and a shippon, which had been farmed by his granddad, Anthony Joy. I took a certain pride in that fact. For me it made Garston Park an extra special place.

Running through the middle of the park was a wide tree-lined tarmac avenue on which every kid in the neighbourhood had learned to ride a bike. This year something strange was happening to the trees. It was still summer but the leaves were already turning yellow and brown. Granddad had said that it was Dutch elm disease, caused by a fungus that had come into this country through Liverpool's docks on timber imported from America and that there were thousands of elm trees in Liverpool that were now dying. 'When it spreads to the rest of the country,' he had said, 'I reckon the landscape of England's cities will change forever.'

Some trees on Garston Park had already started to die. Dad had once peeled off a piece of bark and showed me the spidery pattern of tunnels underneath. He had explained that the elm bark beetle had made these and that it was carrying the fungus from one tree to the next. 'The fungus stops the flow of water through the tree,' he had said, 'and without water the tree dies.'

Other things had been changing in the park recently. The wartime prefabs on Long Lane had now all been demolished. We had relations on Mum's side that used to live there. The bandstand in the centre of the avenue had collapsed and been taken away by the Corpy, and all that remained was a circular flowerbed. The surface of the playground had been tarmacked, but they had left the old concrete flags under the swings.

'To protect the ground from the kids,' the Parky had pontificated to Mum.

'What about protecting the kids from the ground?' Mum had retorted after I had fallen off a swing, smacked and dragged the back of my head on the gravelled concrete flags and she had then spent an hour with a pair of tweezers picking the bits of gravel out of my bloodied scalp.

When we arrived home, Ann and Billy were waiting for us. Since Ann had turned thirteen, we were allowed to be in the house without an adult. On the one hand that was good, because it meant that we did not have to be dragged shopping. On the other hand it was bad, because it meant that Ann was in charge. I hated having an older sister. Like all older sisters she was bossy, plus she was allowed to do things that I was not. I also hated having a younger brother. He messed things up and I was not allowed to do the things that he was not allowed to do. In fact, what I hated most was being in the middle. I always felt that it must be better either to be the youngest or the oldest, rather than being 'piggy in the middle'. Ann was clever at school and she seemed to get all the praise from everyone; I often overheard Mum saying how clever she was. Billy was the baby of the family and he seemed to get all the love from everyone; he was allowed to get away with things that I was never allowed to get away with when I was his age. Being in the middle was definitely not F.A.B.

As we entered the house, Ann presented Mum with the contents of the day's second post. 'Oh! Are there any for me?' I said.

'Those three are addressed to Dad,' Ann reported to Mum. And then, after a pause, she looked at me and added, 'and I've put Dave's stamps to soak in the sink.'

'What?' I exclaimed. Then the surprise was replaced by a stab of anger. 'How dare you! They're nothing to do with you!' I snarled through gritted teeth.

'Now, now,' groaned Mum. 'Don't be like that. She's only trying to help.'

'No she's not,' I argued. 'She's just interfering, being Miss Bossy Boots, sticking her nose in where it doesn't belong.' I turned to Ann. 'Those are my stamps, not yours. I bought them with my pocket money!' I stormed off into the kitchen to see what havoc she had wreaked.

Over my shoulder I heard Mum say softly to Ann, 'You should have left them for him; he wants to do it himself.' What I thought to be a woeful understatement only served to add to my feeling of injustice.

On the kitchen dresser there were five envelopes addressed to me. Each address was written in my handwriting and each envelope contained nothing more than a blank piece of paper. The top right-hand corner of each envelope was missing; the stamps had been cut off. I went to the sink and carefully fished out the five stamps, which had now separated from the pieces of cut envelope. I examined them carefully to make sure Ann had not damaged any of them when she had cut them off and then I checked them to make sure all had been properly franked and cancelled by the Post Office. To my relief they all seemed to be in good condition, but that did not lessen my resentment at Ann's interference.

Mum came into the kitchen to heat up two tins of Heinz vegetable soup for lunch, so I carried my treasures up to my bedroom. I had only just finished drying them with the bath towel when Mum called me to say that the soup was ready. I lined the stamps up on the towel and admired them. They were a set of five, recently issued to commemorate the investiture of the Prince of Wales, which I had saved up for and bought at Tushies' post office. Each of the three 5*d* stamps showed a different view of Caernarfon Castle; the 9*d* stamp showed a Celtic cross; and, the 1*s* stamp carried a portrait of Prince Charles. Although decimal coins were in circulation, we were not due to 'go decimal' for another two years, so stamps were still being issued in pounds, shillings and pence.

'David! Come down now and get this soup before it goes cold,' called Mum.

'Okay, okay, I'm coming.'

'Aye, and so is Christmas,' she chided.

With great care, I lifted the towel and its contents and stowed it in the bottom of the wardrobe, where no one else would find it. I bombed downstairs, taking the steps two at a time. Then, while Mum wasn't looking, I set a new Guinness record for slurping tepid Heinz vegetable soup, before legging it back to my room to retrieve the stamps.

Over the next couple of hours I carefully pressed them, placed them in the airing cupboard to dry and then mounted them on page 73 ('Great Britain – continued') in my copy of the Stanley Gibbons Improved Postage Stamp Album. I enjoyed collecting stamps. There was something intriguing about the artistic detail contained in commemorative stamps and I found it strangely satisfying, seeing them regimentally mounted on page after page of my album. I had received this album for my eighth birthday. It was one of my most prized possessions and one that I kept hidden from Ann and Billy. I kept it hidden from Ann because although we had started collecting stamps at the same time and she had subsequently given it up and had gifted her stamps to me, she would now threaten to take her stamps back whenever we fell out. I kept it hidden from Billy so that he would not mess it up.

While I was waiting for the stamps to dry, I admired the 'On Safari' wall chart mounted above the headboard of my bed. It had a map of the world, showing the location of each of the featured endangered species, and next to each card was a description of the animal; it was the same as the description on the back of the card. I had to admit that the effect was spoiled by the empty space where card No. 8, the leopard, should have been – the card was proving to be almost as rare as the cat.

Later, when I heard Dad coming in, I ran downstairs, eager to show him the freshly mounted additions to my collection. 'Dad! Look at me new stamps,' I urged as he marched into the hall.

'Oh, lovely,' he replied, but without so much as a glance at the album I offered up to him. 'Come on, let's see where they're up to with the moon landing,' he continued as he strode on into the living room.

I felt rebuffed by this apparent lack of interest but I followed him into the living room and sat with the album on my knee. He changed channels to BBC1 and there were Cliff Michelmore, James Burke and Patrick Moore. They were using models of the moon and the spacecraft to illustrate what was happening up in space. Dad listened carefully. I sat in silence. After a minute or so he glanced at me and seemed to notice the stamp album for the first time. 'Which stamps are they?'

'The investiture of the Prince of Wales,' I gushed, with my enthusiasm immediately reignited. I opened the album and handed it to him. This time he lifted his glasses on to his forehead, held the album close to his face and scrutinised the stamps, with just one eye on the television.

'If the moon landing is a success, there's bound to be commemorative stamps issued for that,' he suggested, handing the album back to me. I told him that that would be great. I then began to plan how I could acquire these new stamps without Ann's interference. My thoughts were interrupted by the announcement that the Command/Service Module had successfully entered lunar orbit.

They were counting down to the first ever landing on the moon.

Chapter Five

ON THE SEVENTH DAY

I went up to bed with my head filled with the events of the day. As I lay propped up in bed with my hands behind my head, I reflected on everything that had happened: cycling to the dairy; doing the bottom round, the top round, and the sawdust run; giving Mum a lift in the van; taming The Beast in the crocodile race; seeing the girl in the launderette. That had been a brilliant start to my summer holidays. The only part I tried to forget was being caught by Steven Scales.

The bedroom light went on and in walked Mum, followed by Dad with his arms full of newly ironed clothes, which they then began carefully stacking in the airing cupboard.

'You shouldn't sleep like that,' Mum warned. 'You'll put a strain on your heart.'

'I think I'm too excited to sleep,' I confessed.

'Well, lie on the edge of the bed then,' suggested Dad. 'You'll soon drop off!'

'Har. Har. You're very funny,' I sniped back.

They switched off the light as they left and I snuggled down under the bedclothes.

Before I did finally fall asleep, my dreamy thoughts were about the moon landing. Would it all go according to plan? What would the moon be made of? Would they find any signs of life? What about aliens like in *Dr Who?* – No, I was too old now for that sort of stuff.

When I awoke on Sunday morning I was still filled with that same sense of elation and anticipation. But, I knew that as far as working at the dairy was concerned, I would have to suspend my excitement. For today was Sunday, and on Sundays we had a routine that was different from any other day of the week. It did not involve anyone going to the dairy; instead it involved going to church twice: matins and evensong.

As well as Sundays, we also had routines for other days, plus weekly routines, monthly routines and annual routines. Growing up on a farm, Dad was used to routine and ritual; they had shaped his family life and now they shaped the life of our family. I once asked him why we always kept to planned routines. He just laughed and sang:

I keep six honest serving men

They taught me all I knew.

Their names are What and Why and When

And How and Where and Who.

This sounded like a brilliant answer, but I had no idea what it meant. I did not ask him again; I just followed the routine. Dad worked hard from Monday to Saturday, but Sunday was his day of rest. There was no milk to be delivered and Granddad and Uncle George saw to the needs of the horses. His Sunday routine involved having a lie-in until eight o'clock, before getting up to make his breakfast. Once he had taken the ashes out and built a fresh fire using the new gas grate, he would get the rest of us up for our breakfast. Then, he would take Mum a cup of tea, which she drank in bed.

We had three bedrooms. Mum and Dad had the front bedroom, Billy and I the back bedroom and Ann had the small bedroom to herself. When Dad came in to get me up I was sitting on the bed reading my *TV21* comic; there was a story about a space flight to Mars. I followed Dad downstairs. He had already laid the table with our three Beatles breakfast sets, consisting of a cereal bowl, plate, mug and egg cup. Each item carried the same picture of a smiling Fab Four. He brought me in a soft-boiled egg, which he spooned into my Beatles egg cup, and bread soldiers, which he placed on my Beatles plate. During the week I usually had cornflakes for breakfast, but on Sundays, Dad always made us boiled eggs. He knew how to get a runny yolk just perfect for dipping.

'Go to work on an egg,' he quoted, doing his best Tony Hancock impression.

'More like "Go to church on an egg",' I suggested.

Ann and Billy soon joined me but I made a point of finishing my breakfast before them. I turned the empty eggshell upside-down and placed it back in the egg cup to fool Dad, and then ran back upstairs to claim the bathroom for ten minutes before Ann got in there. Nowadays, her routine in the bathroom seemed to get longer and longer. I knew I could then take my time and finish reading my comic before getting dressed and ready for church; that was my routine.

The annual routines of our lives were influenced by the church calendar – Advent, Christmas, Epiphany, Lent and Easter – with special services dropped in, such as Mothering Sunday, Remembrance Sunday or the Harvest Festival. Being in the choir gave you a sense of the time of year according to what you had been singing in choir practice (routinely, every Wednesday and Friday evening). I particularly enjoyed rehearsing and singing the anthems.

As we left the house, just after ten o'clock, Mum put the Sunday roast in the oven so that it would be ready when we returned; that was her routine. At a quick march we knew we could get to church in about twenty-five minutes. The service did not start until eleven o'clock, but we always had to be there early so that Ann could ring the bells and Billy and I could join the rest of the choirboys in the vestry.

I had never looked forward to walking up and down Chapel Road in my Sunday best. There was always the chance of being spotted by someone from school and then getting skitted on Monday. But I had no such problem now that I had left school. Yet, there was still the chance that Steven Scales would be on his way to Mass. And, as we neared the bottom of Chapel Road, he appeared out of James Street. I avoided making eye contact and just kept looking straight ahead. Even so, as we passed him, I could feel his eyes on me and knew he had that sly, smarmy smile on his face. He was like a fox stalking chickens, biding his time until the farmer was absent; not because he was hungry, but because he enjoyed killing things. In my stomach, the cowardy-custard cabbage whites fluttered frantically.

We arrived at church in plenty of time and the ritual of matins went according to plan and exactly as rehearsed, except that during prayers, the vicar mentioned the three Apollo astronauts: Neil Armstrong, Edwin Aldrin and Michael Collins. We prayed for their safe return to earth. Afterwards, the vestry was filled with excited boyish discussion about the impending moon landing. We knew all of the NASA terminology: LEM, CSA, ELS, EVA, CAPCOM, FIDO etc. I was ever so slightly disappointed that they did not use F.A.B.

Upon our return home, Dad opened the front door and we were greeted by the warm, comforting, mouth-watering smell of a roast dinner, just about ready for the table. The crispy aroma filled the house. We went upstairs to change out of our Sunday clothes while Dad laid the table and Mum prepared to serve up. Sunday lunch was always 'meat and two veg' with a big jug of gravy. That is how Dad had it when he lived at the dairy and that is how we had it now. Each week we had a different roast: lamb, beef, pork, ham or chicken, and it was served with potatoes (either creamed or roasted) and carrots or peas.

When I came back downstairs, Dad had the table laid and he was standing in the middle of the living room watching the television. Our living room seemed sparse compared to that of Nana and Granddad's. We didn't have their old, heavy furniture, though Mum was very proud of her sideboard. Our three-piece suite was made of long metal springs stretched across wooden frames to support the cushions. You could take the cushions off and play tunes by twanging the springs – but I was too old now for that sort of stuff.

Dad was watching the end of *University Challenge*. This was one of his favourite programmes. Because he had left school at such an early age, he did so without any qualifications.

But, in order to be able to help us three kids with our home-work, he had recently attended night school and obtained O Levels in English, Maths and Spanish. So now he could answer *University Challenge* questions on those subjects (when he was doing mental arithmetic he would whistle the calculation through his teeth). He was also good at history – especially good at remembering dates – and, of course, he could answer any question about horses.

As I walked into the living room, Bamber Gascoigne was urging on the proceedings as the clock counted down. 'Fingers on buzzers, your starter for ten, no conferring,' he said.

To my surprise and delight the next question was on the topic of British birds. I knew my birds. For my seventh birthday I was given a copy of *The Observer's Book of Birds*. It described two hundred and forty-three kinds of birds and had a picture on each page. I would read it by covering the name at the top of the page and trying to identify the picture.

'Which British bird is colloquially known as the Bog-Boomer or Bitter-Bum?' Bamber asked.

Buzzzz!

'Kings College, Simmons.'

'Bittern!' I answered.

'The Bittern,' said Kings College, Simmons.

'Correct,' declared Bamber.

'Ayup!' Dad cheered.

'And now, five bonus points for each correct answer: which three British birds are named after towns in the south of England?'

Kings College conferred.

'Err, Dartford Warbler. Errm ... Kentish Plover?' I offered.

'Ha!' Dad laughed.

Kings College had nothing to offer.

'The correct answers are: Kentish Plover, Dartford Warbler and Sandwich Tern,' announced Bamber.

'I didn't know that Sandwich was a place,' I admitted.

'I didn't know that Sandwich was a bird,' confessed Dad. 'Perhaps we should have conferred!' We laughed together. That was the first time I had ever known the answer to a *University Challenge* question. I was well and truly chuffed.

The next programme was also one of Dad's favourites: *All Our Yesterdays*, narrated by Brian Inglis. They were showing archive film footage of Germany launching V1 'Doodlebug' rockets. 'They're the same scientists who have built the Saturn V rocket,' Dad said to no one in particular. He would watch this programme with great concentration and now and again he would make a comment to himself or say the dates aloud before the narrator had the chance.

Ann and Billy joined us and then Mum brought in the first two oven-warmed and fully loaded dinner plates. Dad immediately turned the television off. He usually waited until *All Our Yesterdays* had finished before he switched it off for dinner.

'Aren't you goin' to watch it 'til the end?' I asked him.

'No,' replied Mum, 'we have something to talk about over dinner.'

'About what? Are we going to go to Blackpool after all?' I pleaded.

'No,' she snapped. 'You have been told: we cannot afford to go to Blackpool this year.' Billy began to sulk. 'Now look what you've done. Wait until we're all seated and then we can talk.'

Dad helped Mum to bring in the rest of the meal and then we all sat quietly while the gravy jug was passed around, waiting to hear whatever it was we were going to talk about.

'Right,' said Dad, once he had swallowed his first mouthful. 'I've a little announcement to make. Ahem! We – are buying – a car!'

There was a moment's silence while we took in this new information; it had come right out of the blue. We had never had a car and the idea of getting one had never, ever been mentioned before.

'Wow! What sort of car?' Ann asked.

'We're getting a blue Hillman Imp,' announced Dad proudly and then he gushed, 'I've been having driving lessons for the past couple of months and I have my test booked in four weeks' time. I'm buying the car from my cousin Doug. It used to be his dad's. I've already bought L-plates for it. Granddad is going to sit in with me while I practise for my test. He already has a driving licence.'

'How come Granddad has a driving licence?' I quizzed. 'He doesn't have a car.'

'He's had a licence since he was in the army,' replied Dad. 'In those days you did not need to pass a test. I know he hasn't driven for a long time but his licence means he is qualified to sit in with me while I practise.' He looked at our stunned faces. 'Well, what do you think?'

'Lovely!' Ann said.

'Great!' Billy said.

'F.A.B!' I said.

We ate our dinner while Mum and Dad chatted on about how a car was going to change our lives for the better. I was surprised at how enthusiastic Dad was at the prospect of having a car. It was something that he had never seemed to need, especially with having the horses. Mum seemed to be even more excited than Dad. I could not understand that, seeing as she would not be the one who would be driving it.

Mum always served up too much food for us, yet whenever any of us left food on our plates she would always cajole us saying that there were starving children in Africa who were dying for the want of food like that. Nevertheless, as far as we were aware, none of our leftovers ever found their way to Africa – they usually ended up in a stew later in the week.

Dad cleared away the empty dinner plates and brought out the pudding bowls. For 'afters' Mum always made a rice pudding, cooked in the oven with a brown skin on top. Dad said it was 'to fill the cracks' – and he said that every single time it was served. After a roast dinner and a rice pudding, we were all well and truly stuffed.

As we were not allowed to play out on a Sunday, the routine was for us three kids to settle down and watch the afternoon matinee on the television. Mum and Dad retreated to the kitchen to wash the dishes. After twenty minutes, like clockwork, a cry went up. 'Whey-hey!' shouted Dad, clapping his hands once and then rubbing them together. There followed the usual response from Mum as she screamed 'No! Eric! Eric! No!' and then legged it upstairs, with Dad in hot pursuit, laughing his head off.

When we were younger we thought that Dad was hurting her, and we would leg it after him and hang on to his trousers as he tried to climb the stairs. Then one day Mum and Dad had sat us down and explained that Dad was not doing anything to hurt her. They said that they were playing and, just like we kids did when we played, they laughed and screamed also. So, they said, there was no need for us to be trying to stop him from doing anything because we were just spoiling their fun. I had asked in all innocence if Dad was being 'a dirty old man', but they had both howled at that.

'I'm not old,' Dad had laughed.

'Certainly not too old to chase me upstairs!'

'And certainly not too old to remember what for!' Dad had added, clapping his hands together again and giving up another 'Whey-hey!' The two of them had a good laugh at that and although at the time we did not find it quite as funny as they did, we understood enough to know that 'Whey-hey!' meant adults playing games upstairs. From then onwards whenever the cry went up, we would just look at each other, roll our eyes mouthing the words 'dirty old man' and then just carry on watching the film.

The next event in our Sunday routine was for Dad to reappear and he did so at about half-past four. He would come down and sit with us while we watched the late afternoon drama. It was a regular hour-long series slot, just before teatime. Dad knew most of the stories already so he was able to explain anything that we did not understand. Today we were watching *The Flaxton Boys*. It had a great theme tune (Dad said it was the *Classical Symphony* by Prokofiev). Over the years we had watched such great classics as *Hawkeye and the Last of the Mohicans*, *The Three Musketeers*, *The Man in the Iron Mask*, *The Count of Monte Cristo* and *Tom Brown's Schooldays*. They were great stories and when we were younger we used to act them out – but I was too old now for that sort of stuff.

After the drama had finished there was a news bulletin, confirming that the moon landing would be attempted later in the evening. Dad said that we would be back from church in time to see the television coverage. He walked briskly into the kitchen to help Mum prepare tea.

Ann wandered into the front room, switched on the Dansett Bermuda and put on her Bob Dylan LP, which she had been given for her last birthday. Dad heard the opening chords of 'The Times They Are A-changin', and propped open the front room door so that we could all listen to the song. When it came to the chorus, the three of us stood in the hall and chimed in together. We could hear Dad singing in the kitchen, doing his best nasal impersonation of Bob Dylan – 'for the times, they are a-changin'.

'"Changin'"! "Changin'"?' called Mum. 'It's Change-ing.'

But then we showed her the printed lyrics – ha!

At evensong we prayed again for the astronauts and the vicar cut short his sermon so that everyone could get home in time to catch the moon landing. It was to be on the nine o'clock news, which they extended to cover the event.

This time when we arrived home, it was the smell of the seaside that greeted us. Mum had left a pan of 'kewins' (or winkles) to simmer while we were out. She put them into a colander and gave us each a pin to winkle them out of their shells. They looked like bogeys, but tasted much nicer. We ate them gathered around the television.

We could see Houston mission control and could hear their communications with the astronauts. James Burke explained to us what was happening. It all seemed to be taking ages. There was obviously some concern about the amount of fuel, yet the voices of the astronauts sounded very calm. Then we heard the words 'the Eagle has landed' and a caption came up on the screen saying 'Man on the Moon'.

'That's it, they're down,' announced Dad. There was applause at mission control and we all joined in.

The presenters announced that the moonwalk was going to happen earlier than had originally been planned. It would be taking place just after three o'clock in the morning. They said that it would be 'the most thrilling event in broadcasting history', a 'historic landmark' and a 'momentous occasion'. They also announced that there would be live pictures from the moon's surface and that there would be continuous broadcasting right through the night.

'That's the first time we've ever had an all-night broadcast,' commented Dad.

'Can't we stay up to watch the moonwalk?' Ann pleaded.

'Yeah, can we?' Billy enthused.

'Yeah. We don't have any school to get up for,' I pointed out.

'No,' replied Mum. 'It's too late and you'll never stay awake that long.'

'Yeah we will,' I protested. 'It's the first man on the moon! We're too excited to sleep!'

'I'm not having Billy stay up that late.'

'Well, he can go to bed then,' I argued.

'I'm not goin' to bed,' insisted Billy. 'I wanna see it too.'

'There you are,' concluded Mum, as if that had made her point. 'You can all go to bed now and then watch it on the news in the morning.'

Berloody Billy! He was like an anchor on all my aspirations. 'But that won't be the same!' I objected. 'It's ... it's ... the most thrilling event in broadcasting history,' I managed with a touch of initiative.

'Yeah. An historic landmark,' said Ann.

'And a mental-old-cajun,' added Billy.

'A momentous occasion,' corrected Dad, laughing.

Faced with this unified plea, Mum decided to defer the matter to Dad. His solution was that we should all go to bed now, to get some sleep and he would put an alarm clock in Ann's room, set for three o'clock. She could then wake us two boys and we could all go down and watch the moonwalk together.

And that is exactly what we did. It was a bit of an adventure in itself, getting up in the middle of the night without the adults present. We got ourselves downstairs. There were only the cold ashes of last night's fire in the grate, so Billy and I snuggled up on the couch to keep warm. Ann turned the television set on. We counted down, waiting for the set to warm up. Eventually, we had a picture. It was the same picture of mission control that we had seen before we went to bed. We talked with our eyes glued to the set.

'Me dad said that they might do commemorative stamps of the moonwalk,' I remarked.

'Miss Astley said they'd do them in America but not in Britain,' Billy commented.

'Who's Miss Astley?' Ann asked him.

'A student teacher we've been having. She brought her collection of first day covers in to school to show us. She knows what stamps are going to be issued this year.'

'What's a "first day cover"?' I asked.

'It's like a special envelope with the new stamps on, which is posted on the first day that the stamps are issued. She gets them sent to her by the Post Office. They look beautiful.'

I took my eyes away from the screen and looked at Billy. I was dumbstruck at his knowledge, that he should know something about stamps that I did not.

'I didn't know you liked stamps,' admitted Ann.

'Neither did I,' I added.

'Yous never asked,' retorted Billy.

'If I'd have known, you could have had my old album,' said Ann.

'I know, but you never asked me. You just gave it to Dave,' he said, with just a hint of accusation.

Ann seemed to be as taken aback by this revelation as I did. Then, as if she had come to a decision, she left the room. Billy and I stared at the screen in silence. When Ann returned, she was holding her old stamp album. It was just a soft-backed beginner's album. There were no stamps in it because I had put them all into my collection. She handed the album to Billy. 'Here, you can have this if you want. I was sure I hadn't thrown it out after Dave had finished with it.'

'Oh! Thanks Ann!' Billy replied.

We returned to watching the screen – still mission control. Out of the corner of my eye I could see Billy flicking through the empty pages of the stamp album. I supposed that I was expected to give him Ann's stamps. But there was no way I was going to do that. She had given me the 1*s* 9*d* Gipsy Moth IV, the 5*d* QE2 and the 4*d* Concorde – they were all irreplaceable. Nevertheless, it bothered me. I felt obliged to do something.

Then I had a brainwave. I legged it upstairs to find my album and returned immediately, holding an envelope. I handed it to Billy. 'That's me swaps envelope. You can take what stamps you want from that,' I offered, as casually as I could manage.

'Wow! Thanks, Dave,' Billy replied, sounding quite astonished at this act of kindness. This felt like the right thing to do, the adult thing to do; it made me feel good. Ann looked over and gave a smile of approval. For a rare moment, the three of us all wore smiles of our own making; it made quite a change from our usual squabbling. Then our attention was grabbed by James Burke saying that we were about to see the first ever live pictures from the moon; he said the pictures were from a camera mounted on the outside of the LEM (Lunar Excursion Module).

The black and white image was very fuzzy, almost blurred. Ann tried adjusting the contrast and brightness dials, but it made no difference. She then tried changing channels but they were all broadcasting the same picture. I turned off the living room light in order to see the picture better. The glow of the screen filled the room with an eerie light.

We watched in silence as a ghostly figure appeared from the top left-hand corner of the screen. It was Neil Armstrong, climbing down the ladder on the leg of the LEM. He seemed to take a lifetime to get ready to step off the craft and on to the surface of the moon. Eventually, he did it. 'That's one small step for man – one giant leap for mankind.'

'F.A.B.,' I whispered.

Chapter Six

THE THREE MUSKETEERS

We watched the moonwalk until the astronauts climbed the ladder and returned to the LEM to sleep. We climbed the stairs and returned to our beds to do likewise. Dad woke me later to see if I wanted to go with him to the dairy once again. Despite my lack of sleep, I volunteered without hesitation.

Together with Uncle George, we did the two rounds and then Dad and I spent the rest of the morning restacking the hay bales, which had been delivered while we were out. The deliverymen had just stacked the new bales on top of the old ones, but Dad did not like things that way. He was concerned that the old bales would go stale and rot at the bottom of the stack.

'First in, first out,' he instructed. So, we restacked the bales with the old ones on top. Our stack was huge. It looked like The Tower of Babel in the Children's Illustrated Bible. It was dry, dusty and thirsty work and I was grateful when Granddad came into the shippon to tell us that dinner was ready.

Granddad was Musketeer 'Perce-os'. At eighty years of age he was already well past retirement age and did not drive the horses any more. He was not a tall man; he would have been about five feet tall in his prime. But now there was a bend forming at the top of his spine, which was causing him to hunch over, and this made him appear even shorter. He said it was due to spending most of his life sitting on a stool, bent over, milking cows.

He always wore a full three-piecer with a collar and tie. His own variation on this theme was to wear a trilby over his neat silver hair. He called the trilby his 'cowboy hat'. He claimed it was a gift from Buffalo Bill and Annie Oakley, who he met as a child, when they brought their Wild West Show to Liverpool in 1903. He also wore a pair of black dress shoes. They were so shiny and clean that you could see your face in them and they seemed to stay that way no matter what work he did: serving the customers, grooming the horses or even mucking out.

He was never to be seen without his pipe. It was either in his mouth or in his right hand or somewhere in between, but in the stables it was never lit as it was a fire hazard. He cleaned it using feathers shed from Uncle George's pigeons, and they were black with tar when he had finished with them. In one pocket of his waistcoat (he pronounced it 'westkut') he carried a tobacco pouch and in the other a box of Pilot matches that were made at the 'matchwerks', in Garston. Most of the time his head was surrounded by a cloud of pipe smoke and the scent of that aromatic tobacco followed him everywhere. His one other vice was his sweet tooth. In his jacket pocket there was usually a piece of foil, carefully folded around either a piece of Milk Aero or a piece of Fry's Chocolate Cream, depending which took his fancy on the day. On his left hand were four fingers and a stump. He had lost the top half of his thumb in a turnip-chopping machine after he returned from fighting in the First World War, but he never spoke about the war and I knew not to ask. He was married to Ellen, my nana, who was even shorter than he was.

'There's a plate of chips awaiting you both,' he announced.

Chips! At home we had fish and chips for tea on Fridays, but to have them for a dinner was something of a treat. I left the shippon at a gallop.

'Don't be rushin',' warned Granddad.

'Okay – I'll be English,' I called back over my shoulder. I ran through to the dairy and the moreish smell grew stronger. There was something so delicious about the smell of chip-shop chips. From mid-morning onwards, tendrils of that wonderful bouquet would float through the streets, seductively caressing the nostrils, tempting everyone to come to the fish and chip shop. Later in the day, that mouth-watering aroma would meet and mingle with the odour of burning coal descending from every chimney pot. Chips and coal fires – that was the smell of Garston. It was a homely smell.

I dashed up the steps into the kitchen. Nana was lifting two warm plates from the oven. The chips were on the dresser, still wrapped in newspaper. 'Ah, there you are,' she said. 'Wash your hands and I'll put these on the table for you.' Dad came in behind me. We stood at the kitchen sink, taking it in turns to scrub our hands with a block of green carbolic soap and then we followed our noses into the living room. With the polished wood of its fireplace, dresser and bureau, with the brass of its many ornaments and with the dark leather of its three-piece suite, it looked just like the living room of a dairy should look. By the window overlooking the covered yard was a sturdy wooden dining table, and on it were two plates of steaming chips and a third piled high with buttered bread.

'You'll both be ready for this, then,' smiled Nana.

'I'll say,' agreed Dad, 'we've done a full morning's work and then some.' I was chuffed with this recognition of my contribution. As we sat ourselves down, Dad addressed the room in general. 'And what time do chips get up in the morning?' he prompted.

'Chips get up potato clock!' was my well-rehearsed response.

'Ha! That's right,' he laughed, giving a clap of his hands and then rubbing them together in eager anticipation of the meal to come. With that, we both tucked in, Dad using a fork and me making chip butties. Nana left to make a pot of tea for Dad. I asked him if, like me, he had worked in the dairy when he was only eleven years old. I knew the answer to this, but I asked anyway, just to hear him talk.

'I was much younger than eleven when I started working,' he explained, between alternate mouthfuls of chips and bread. 'I was born in this house and my earliest memory is working in the fields with me papa. At that time much of the land in Garston was farmland and the Joys were just one of the families who farmed it. I spent every day of my life either in the fields, or milking the cows or out with the horses delivering milk ...'

I folded the bread over a handful of chips and then squashed the butty flat before taking the biggest mouthful I could cope with.

'... and I was not at all happy when I had to leave that life and go to school. I used to sit in class and listen to the horse-drawn tradesmen passing the school on Island Road. I could identify each one by the sound of the horse's hooves. School was okay and I enjoyed learning but I wanted to be back on the farm. I didn't have many friends of my own age because I'd grown up an only son working every day with my family. So, I left school when I was fourteen. That was the earliest you could leave in those days. I carried on working here until my call up came through, and I joined the army.'

Nana came in with a pot of tea. She caught the end of what Dad was saying. 'And your granddad was not at all happy at the idea of your dad going to war,' she said to me. 'He would rather have gone himself than send Eck.'

'Whywasdat?' I mumbled, with a mouthful of chip butty.

'Because,' explained Dad, 'your granddad fought in the trenches in the First World War and he thought the Second World War was going to be the same. He saw many of his comrades fall and he didn't want me to have to go through that. But, fortunately for me, there wasn't any more trench warfare ...'

I squashed another butty. I loved the way the hot chips melted the butter on the bread. I licked it up as it ran down my fingers.

'... I was originally in The Manchesters and I was waiting to cross the English Channel to fight in France. But when the boats returned to pick us up, they were full of wounded soldiers because the Dunkirk evacuation had begun. I was transported back to the north-west and was transferred to the Veterinary Corp. I made some good friends in the Vets, some of whom I'm still in touch with to this very day. We spent most of our time working on farms in Lancashire.'

'How come you was working on farms if you was a soldier?'

'Well, there was nowhere to send us to fight because we couldn't cross the Channel. Plus, we needed to grow as much food as possible because there was very little coming into the country. So, the best use of soldiers was to have us working the land as part of the war effort. But as soon as I was on leave I came straight back to Garston to work on the family farm. In fact, there were plenty of times when I'd arrive home and go straight out on the milk round in my army fatigues.' He paused to pour his tea.

'How come we don't still have cows now then?'

'Because, after the war, land was needed for house building and all the farmland in Garston was built on. So there was no more dairy herd. In fact we took the last hay crop off Joy's Field in 1958, the year that you were born. The milk rounds were all reallocated but we were able to keep the milk delivery side of the family business. We continued working out of Wellington Dairy and we were able to keep the horses because we still had the stables and shippon.'

'And you became Eric the Milkman,' I said.

'Aye, that's me,' he laughed.

We carried on talking our way through our lunch. Dad loved to talk – to me, to the customers, to the horses, to himself. I liked it when he reminisced and told stories about his childhood. He was the only surviving representative of his generation of Joys. Consequently, while he was growing up, his elders were his only role models and he was very much a chip off the old block. On the other hand, he embraced the modern world with gusto. In his own way he straddled the generations and was quite comfortable doing so. He claimed he had the best of both worlds – a mixture of the past and present.

Dad was Musketeer 'Eck-amis' (or, Eric-amiss, he would say) and he was fifty years old. Height was not an abundant characteristic in the Joy family gene pool; none of us would ever wind the Liver clocks. Dad stood at five feet four inches. In his own words, he was spared the indignity of being the runt of the litter only by the fact that, being an only child, there was no litter. He wore glasses, had a slight squint and had ears that stood out at right angles to his head, like ruddy gas taps. He would swear that when he cycled down Chapel Road, his 'flappers' gave him lift. He put his ears down to the fact that he had grown up wearing a cap, but I only had to look in the mirror to work out that they were the result of nature rather than nurture. Dad's three-piecer was supplemented by a flat cap or occasional trilby and by a pair of brown lace-up army boots topped with bicycle clips. He cycled to and from work and when it was raining he wore a sou'wester and cape, giving the appearance of a tent on wheels. He kept his bicycle clips on all day, whether he was cycling or not. Mum claimed he did not even take them off to go to bed.

He always seemed to be happy. 'Joy by name, Joy by nature,' was his motto. He would whistle a tune as he went about his work and he took pride in keeping up to date with popular music. As a family, every Thursday evening we would watch *Top of the Pops* on our black and white television set. Like everyone else in Liverpool, we took great pride in the Beatles and for Christmas, Mum and Dad would buy us their latest 45 rpm single to play on our portable Dansett Bermuda record player. Dad could often be heard whistling a tune by the Beatles, or for that matter, by Vera Lynn or by Prokofiev – a mixture of traditional and contemporary.

He also had an irrepressible sense of humour. But, it was the sense of humour of a soldier and of a farmer, so at times it was a bit coarse to say the least; often to do with bodily functions. This had never gone down very well with Mum:

'That's NOT funny, Eric Joy. You're a dirty old man!'

'I'm not old!'

For 'afters' we both had a buttered iced bun from Sayers. I used to love turning the top of mine upside down so that the icing would mix with the butter – but I was too old now for that sort of stuff. Dad poured his tea into his saucer to cool it and slurped it from there to swill down his iced bun. Once we had finished, we washed our hands and walked back to the stable yard.

I was looking forward to an afternoon working with Dad. We had not discussed what work we were going to do but, once the rounds were completed, there was always something to be done in the stables. You could say that Dad was a DIY enthusiast, but not the domestic kind; not putting up shelves, decorating, wiring, plumbing or anything like that. No, Dad worked with leather, with metal and with wood. A harness is made of leather and metal; carts and floats are made of metal and wood. Dad had grown up learning how to repair and maintain all of these. He rarely bought any components; he made them himself from whatever was at hand.

So, I wondered, what would it be today? Cleaning the harness? Spokeshaving a new set of shafts? Whitewashing the walls? Painting the float? Pumping up the van's tyres? Grooming the horses?

We walked into the stable yard. 'Right,' I said, rubbing my hands together, 'warra we doing now?'

'Well, later we'll take Peggy up to the smithy, but right now there's some muckinout needs doing.'

'Muckinout? Oh! Erm ... what's Uncle George doin'?'

'He's got some birds in a race this afternoon.'

'Has he?' I enthused.

Dad smiled. 'Would you like to go and watch them come home?'

'Well, as long as you don't mind muckinout without me?'

'No, I'm sure I'll manage somehow,' he laughed. 'I'll come and get you when I've got Peggy ready.'

'Great. I'll seeya later.'

I skipped back into the jigger and followed it to the large green wooden back door of No. 39 Wellington Street; the home of Uncle George and Aunty Mary.

Great Uncle George was Granddad's brother – and he was Musketeer 'George-os' ('Gorgeous George-os', according to Aunty Mary). He was seventy-six years old and Dad said he had never missed a day's work in his entire life. He topped out at five feet ten inches, which was tall for a Joy. His rough-hewn face always sported at least a day's growth of grey stubble. On his head grew a thin covering of grey hair that looked like a random hen had just finished scratching around in it. This was often hidden beneath a flat cap. His variation on the three-piecer was a buttoned-up dark grey westkut over a collarless pin-striped shirt, which he always wore with the sleeves rolled up to his elbows; a pair of thick-weave dark grey pants that were tucked in to a pair of leather chaps; and, on his feet, a pair of clogs. These clogs had alder wood soles with leather uppers and they made his feet look disproportionately large; Dad said that they were so large he should hire them out for gondolas in Venice. The hollow clunk they made meant that you could always hear when he was coming.

Whilst Uncle George talked very little and laughed even less, Aunty Mary was quite the opposite. She had a Gaelic lilt to her accent and she would cluck away like one of Uncle George's hens. Whenever any of us grandchildren would visit, she would love to make a fuss; and, to be honest, we loved her for making a fuss. (We used to sing: 'Aunty Mary had a canary up the leg of her drawers, She pulled it down for half-a-crown and sold it to Santa Clause' – but I was too old now for that sort of stuff).

Carefully, I pushed the back door open so as not to disturb any birds that might be waiting to come down. The door made a trundling noise. Uncle George had rigged up a lead counter-weight, which, through a system of pullies, ensured that the back door closed to, all by itself. I peeped around the door to make sure the coast was clear.

Uncle George was an enthusiastic breeder and racer of pigeons, or 'racing homers' as they were called. Running the full length of the back yard was his pride and joy – a row of green and white striped pigeon lofts. I could see that the loft doors were open but that Uncle George was sitting in the house eating his dinner. Aunty Mary heard the trundle of the pullies and looked out. Through the dining room window, she waved me to come in. I walked up the yard, past the open pigeon loft. Whenever you walked into the yard you were greeted by a symphony of cooing and the fluttering whine of flapping wings. I turned into the small glass lean-to that led to the kitchen steps and I was immediately aware of a strong earthy scent, which came from a jungle of fuchsias.

This was Aunty Mary's pride and joy. The lean-to had two rows of shelves and every inch of shelf and floor was taken up by a pot of fuchsias. These beautiful pendant bell-shaped flowers filled the lean-to from red-tiled floor to glass-paned ceiling. They came in many shapes: bushed, trailing, pyramidal and tree-like. And they came in a variety of colours: white, mauve, violet, cream, red and pink, sometimes with two or three colours on a single bloom. Their long stamens and stigma, hanging like suspended raindrops, provided an irresistible attraction for bees, which now filled the space of the lean-to with industrious buzzing.

'Heloo, Heloo, me dear. Come on in, won't you,' cooed Aunty Mary from the dining room as I climbed the kitchen steps, like Dr Livingstone emerging from the jungle. On the steps were half a dozen large, square, wooden boxes, each with a sealed clock on the front. These were the racing clocks. They had a slot in the top into which you placed the rubber ring once you had removed it from the incoming racing pigeon's leg. Once the ring was inserted, the clock recorded the time and the box could not be opened again by anyone except the race organisers.

The living room was dominated by a huge fireplace-oven combination. It was made of black cast iron with brass trimmings and it had a red-tiled hearth; it smelled of black lead and Brasso. When we were younger we used to pretend it was the witch's oven in *Hansel and Gretel* – but I was too old now for that sort of stuff.

I walked in just as Uncle George was leaving the table. Aunty Mary gave me one of her fussy hugs. 'George is just going out to call his birds down. Do you want to come in and watch from the window?'

'Yes please!' I sat myself at the table, overlooking the yard.

Uncle George appeared carrying the wooden clocks and he placed them inside the open door of the loft. He retired to the doorway of the lean-to, gave his nose another good blow on his handkerchief rag and then stood looking up at the sky. In his hand he now held a tin scoop full of seed. He stood watching for about five minutes and then he shook the scoop and called out. 'Come on. Come on.' The seed rattled metallically.

'They'll be sitting on the roof of the house,' mused Aunty Mary. 'He'll be needing to get them down quick if he's to have any chance of winning.'

I could picture the birds perched on the gutter of the house casually peering down at the backyard, blissfully unaware of the urgency of the situation. The clocks were ticking and every second counted but Uncle George managed to keep any sign of concern or frustration from his voice. 'Come on, come on,' he called again and threw some seed into the loft, where it bounced noisily on the wooden floor. With that, two pigeons came into view and landed on the roof of the loft. They then flew down onto the concrete floor of the yard and pecked about at a few seeds. Uncle George did not move. The clocks were ticking. We waited inside with bated breath. Then, first one and then the other bird flew into the open loft door. Uncle George smoothly stepped across the yard and followed them into the loft, closing the door behind him.

'Gottem!' cheered Aunty Mary. 'That'll be a good time. He'll be pleased with that.'

The loft door swung open again and Uncle George climbed out, carrying two of the clocks. As he carried them over to the lean-to, his face showed no sign of emotion. He placed the clocks on the kitchen steps and then returned to his position in the doorway to continue his vigil of the sky. Over the next ten minutes another two birds returned and the sequence of enticement, capture, de-ringing and clocking-in was repeated.

'The last two don't really matter now,' said Aunty Mary. 'This is their first race so they're not yet used to the routine. He only entered them to give them the practice.' After another ten minutes of inactivity, she called out to Uncle George. 'Any sign of them yet?'

'Aye, they're on the roof,' he replied.

'You can go out and have a look if you want,' she suggested. I left the table and joined Uncle George in the lean-to.

'There,' he said to me, pointing up at the roof of the house. I could see two heads bobbing around at the edge of the gutter, as if they were discussing whether or not they should fly down. Uncle George threw another scoopful of seed into the loft and that seemed to make their minds up for them. They both launched themselves from the rooftop and flapped their wings to parachute themselves to the ground. But, as we watched, the birds seemed to baulk as if they had had second thoughts. And, out of the sky, high above the Duke of Wellington Hotel, there appeared a black shape moving at an incredible speed, like a dive-bomber, and getting bigger by the second. It intercepted one of the pigeons and there was a silent explosion of feathers. Slightly larger than the pigeon, the shape seemed to be wrestling with its catch as it tumbled onwards, over our heads, down towards the river, disappearing from our sight behind the glass roof of the lean-to and the jungle of fuchsias. As I looked up I noticed that a new bloom had appeared at the top of the fuchsia canopy – a single blood-red raindrop.

It had all happened in seconds. There was a small shower of feathers in the yard. The lighter downy feathers floated gently in descent while a couple of heavier wing feathers helicoptered down like sycamore seeds. 'Aye!' swore Uncle George and abruptly broke the spell. We rushed out into the yard to look back over the lean-to roof to see where the dive-bomber was going, but it was beyond my view.

'What was it?' I gasped as I recovered my senses.

'A berloody falcon,' he swore, still gazing over the roof of the lean-to with his hand up to shade his eyes. 'It's comin' down in the goodsies.'

'Wow!' I exclaimed, open-mouthed. I then realised that this was not something to be too ecstatic about.

Aunty Mary came to the kitchen door. 'What happened?'

'A falcon took one of the pigeons,' I informed her, trying hard not to erupt with the excitement at what I had just witnessed. I had seen this sort of thing on the natural history programmes on the television, but never in real life. Wow! It was breathtaking. I wanted to shout about it.

'Is that right, George?' she asked, incredulously.

'Aye. The dockers said that there's a pair nesting in one of the cranes. It must have been one of them.'

Aunty Mary joined us in the yard. The three of us looked at the sky. The final few feathers floated down. There was no sign of the other pigeon. 'I'll be surprised if that last one will come down now,' muttered Uncle George.

'What'll happen to it?' I asked him.

'It'll just go feral and join all those other pigeons you see in the streets.'

'So, what sort of falcon was it then?' I enquired, as matter-of-factly as possible.

'Probably a peregrine.'

'Of course! A peregrine falcon!' I felt a little embarrassed for not realising that that's what it was, but I was also impressed that Uncle George did.

'That's not usual though,' said Aunty Mary. 'Is it, George?'

'Seeing a peregrine is not usual nowadays, what with all these pesticides. But, killing pigeons? Aye, that's usual enough. Racing pigeons have been bred from rock doves that live on coastal cliffs. That's where the peregrine usually takes them from. It stoops from high up and flies faster than a hundred miles an hour. It kills pigeons instantly when it hits them. There are plenty of feral birds down at the docks. Let's just hope it sticks to those in future and leaves my birds alone.'

That was the most I had heard Uncle George say in one go; in fact, it was the most I had heard him say in any given week. I knew he shared my interest in natural history, but he was like a lead door-weight when it came to squeezing information from him.

'But there's no cliffs around here,' I pointed out.

'Aye,' he agreed, 'I s'pose things are a changin' out in the wild as well as everywhere else and the peregrine is having to adapt like the rest of us.'

He did not seem to be overly concerned about the lost bird, but then it was always difficult to tell with Uncle George. Maybe he was still pleased about getting two birds back early. He continued to stare up at the sky.

'Better get the clocks ready for collection,' suggested Aunty Mary.

'Aye,' he replied. He closed the loft door, picked up two of the clocks and carried them through the kitchen to the front of the house. The race organisers would collect them and Uncle George would then have to wait for the results to be announced.

'I'm going to go and tell me dad what just happened,' I gushed to Aunty Mary.

'Right you are, luvvie. Come back and see us again soooon,' she cooed.

'F.A.B.'

Chapter Seven

THE SMITHY

I ran into the stable yard just as Dad was bringing Peggy out of the shippon. 'You'll never guess what I just seen!' I called, and then began a blow-by-blow account of what had happened to Uncle George's pigeons. As I talked, we hitched Peggy to the float. Dad oohed, aahed and laughed at my excited narrative, which I continued as we set off for the smithy.

Our local smithy, Vanstone's, was in Woolton Quarry. As well as being a blacksmith, working with metal and machine, Bernard Vanstone was also a farrier, working with hoof and shoe. Woolton Quarry was the name given to an area of Woolton, but the smithy was located quite literally in the quarry. The yard was at the end of Mill Street, which sloped steeply down to the quarry floor. The red sandstone had been used in the construction of many large buildings in Liverpool, including the spectacular cathedral – the Anglican one, that is, not 'Paddy's Wigwam'. Now, the sheer sides of the defunct quarry provided the smithy with a similarly spectacular cathedral-like backdrop, which was only slightly spoiled by the huge towers of car tyres stacked in the quarry like giant liquorice allsorts.

We always used the milk float for trips to the smithy. It was the lightest of our vehicles and the journey to Woolton, along Woolton Road, was an 'up-hill-and-down-dale' affair. We passed Garston cenotaph and then dropped under the railway bridge at Allerton station. This marked the boundary between Garston and the neighbouring district of Allerton. To remove any lingering doubt as to our whereabouts, we then passed Allerton Cemetery, Allerton Hall, Allerton Priory and Allerton Towers on our way to Woolton. This broad swathe of interconnected green space had contributed to the area being known as 'a leafy part of Liverpool'. The entire journey from Garston to Woolton was along a dual carriageway with a wide tree-lined central reservation. At the Garston end, many of these trees were elms, and they were already showing signs of decline. They contrasted sharply with the magnificent beech trees at the Woolton end. These giant structures with their rich deep green foliage stretched so high that they seemed to be supporting the sky.

The top of Woolton Road, at its junction with Menlove Avenue, marked the boundary between Allerton and Woolton. We approached these traffic lights at a slow walk. It was then that we noticed the lights were not working. A single policeman standing in the centre of the junction was controlling the traffic. It was a big junction; the crossroads of two dual carriageways. All traffic in our carriageway had passed us, so Peggy pulled right up to the lights. From there we watched the policeman at work.

He emptied each carriageway in turn; at least, that is what he appeared to do. But we were sure at one point that he had all the left-turning traffic in all carriageways moving at once. When he was ready he would halt the flow of traffic from one carriageway and then turn to the next and repeat the process, but always adaptable to whatever little varia-tions were presented to him. He moved with a certain kind of smoothness and the confidence of someone who was totally in control of the situation. It was like watching a maestro conducting an orchestra; or rather, four orchestras, all at once. I commented on his skill.

'Aye. You used to see that all the time before there were traffic lights,' Dad reminisced, as he put the reins into his right hand and held his left hand up by his shoulder, palm facing forward; in the absence of indicators, this told the policeman that we intended to proceed straight ahead. The policeman spotted this variation on the norm at once. He called us on and held up all the other traffic to give a walking horse all the time it needed to clear the junction. He watched us progress with a big smile on his face, which turned into a laugh when Dad doffed his cap and called out 'thank you' to him.

We turned up Vale Road and then up Castle Street, before crossing Quarry Street into Mill Lane. In this narrow cobbled street I held Peggy while Dad walked to the smithy gates to check if the farrier was available and whether or not there was a queue of horses. There was just one horse being seen to, so we unhitched Peggy and walked her down into the yard, leaving the float resting on its shafts.

Bernard Vanstone was not just a farrier, he was a hot shoe farrier. The forge stood in an open sided lean-to shed.

Despite the shed being open to the elements, the heat of the forge filled the space beneath the rusty corrugated tin roof. You simply had to cross the threshold of the shed to walk into instant warmth that smelled of coal with a hint of metal. On the back wall of the shed hung every possible size and style of steel horseshoe, at least four of each. We stood in the yard with Peggy and waited our turn. As we waited, Mr Vanstone Senior approached us.

Although I addressed him as 'Mr Vanstone', I referred to him in the third person as 'Old Mr Vanstone'. I had met Old Mr Vanstone on many occasions before. When I was younger, I would scour the smithy yard floor for spare horseshoe nails until I held a fistful. Old Mr Vanstone would give me a thrupenny dodger for them – but I was too old now for that sort of stuff. I always found him to be a quiet, softly spoken old man and I enjoyed talking to him. His son, on the other hand, was quite the opposite. Bernard frightened me. I always felt like he was shouting or growling at me. Dad said it was because he had to talk to horses like that to show them who was boss, and then sometimes he forgot to change back to normal talking when speaking to people; he still frightened me.

'Mornin', Eric. Mornin', young'un,' Old Mr Vanstone greeted us. He placed his hand on my shoulder. 'And how are things with thee, young man?' I told him I was working with Dad this summer and that I was going to be learning all about the job. 'Is that right?' He smiled, glancing at Dad, who nodded in agreement. 'Well then, what do you know about shoeing a horse?'

'I've seen it all done before, but I don't know about all the different things that happen,' I explained.

'Right then', he decided, 'I'll explain it to thee while Bernard is shoeing Peggy, shall I?'

'Yes, please,' I accepted his kind offer. We watched in silence while Bernard finished off the horse he was working on. I enjoyed talking with adults, it made me feel special. I wanted to say something to keep the conversation going. 'Danny's gone lame,' I proffered.

'Is that right?' He asked with genuine interest, raising his eyebrows at Dad, who gave a resigned smile and nod in acknowledgement. 'Have you mentioned it to Bernard?' Dad said no, he had not. 'You should do. He'll want to know,' he suggested. Dad nodded again.

When it was our turn, Dad led Peggy into the shed. 'First he'll check all the shoes to see what's required,' said Old Mr Vanstone. Bernard inspected each of Peggy's hooves. To do this, he bent over and grabbed the feather of the leg in question whilst leaning into the horse to encourage it to shift its weight and lift the hoof. He barked out the instruction 'Lift!' and Peggy obliged. With the horse behind him, he held the foot between his knees with the hoof resting on his thighs. From that position he could bend forward and inspect or work on the lower surface of the hoof. A thick flame-proof leather apron protected his chest and midriff. It then split into a pair of chaps to protect his thighs.

Old Mr Vanstone took me by the elbow and we stepped forward to look at one of the hooves as Bernard inspected it. 'The outside of the hoof is called the "wall" and it's very hard,' he said, 'but the underside is a bit softer.' He pointed out the 'sole' and the heart-shaped 'frog' on the underside of the hoof. 'The horse can't feel anything that Bernard does. It's a bit like having your toenails cut,' he explained. We stepped back.

Bernard declared that Peggy only needed her hind shoes replacing. Dad agreed and the farrier set to work. It was fascinating to watch the shoeing process. Old Mr Vanstone described and explained each of the activities to me. Using a buffer and hammer, Bernard straightened the old nails, or clinches, which had been bent over to hold the shoe in place. He loosened the old shoe using a pair of pincers, before pulling out the old nails with the claw of the hammer and then removing the old shoe. He trimmed the wall of the hoof using a pair of nippers and then trimmed away at the sole and frog of the hoof using a drawing knife. Some big chunks of dirty hoof flew from the end of the knife exposing a fresh, creamy white colour beneath. Old Mr Vanstone picked up a piece and showed it to me. I held it in my hand and it felt like rubbery wax. He said with some pride that trimming the hoof in this way was a very skilled task and that if it was not done correctly it would place stress on the legs and cause lameness. I asked him if he had been a farrier. 'Aye,' he replied, 'me fayther taught me and I taught Bernard. But we all did our proper training with the Worshipful Company of Farriers.' I thought he was joking when he announced the last bit, but he didn't laugh. I wondered why they were called 'worshipful'; perhaps it was because they were always bending down.

The next part of the process was my favourite: hot shoeing. Bernard selected a shoe from the back of the shed and held it up to the hoof to check the size. He then placed the shoe in the forge and buried it under the red hot coals. Old Mr Vanstone said that this was to make the metal shoe softer so that it could be altered to better fit the horse's hoof.

He said that every horse was different and did different work at different times in different places. Part of the art of the farrier was to make sure the horse had the correct shoe.

Peggy waited. She rested the toe of her shoeless hoof on the ground but kept her weight on her other three legs. When the shoe was glowing red hot, Bernard thrust a pritchel through the last of its seven nail holes and lifted it out of the forge. Taking the hoof between his thighs once more, he placed the red-hot shoe onto the newly trimmed surface. The shoe hissed and spat as it burned into the hoof, but his leather chaps protected him from the heat.

'Peggy can't feel anything,' Old Mr Vanstone assured me. 'This is to see how well the shoe is fitting and what alterations need to be made. Bernard will be able to tell from the burn mark left on the hoof.' A stream of grey smoke rose into Bernard's face and he puffed his cheeks to blow it away. The smoke filled the air with a most curious smell, which I always found to be both satisfying and yet, disturbing. It was certainly the smell of something cooking but not a smell I had ever encountered in any kitchen.

Bernard removed the hot shoe. If it was held on the hoof for too long it could injure the horse. He examined the burn mark to check for fit, made a mental note of what adjustment was necessary and then put the shoe back into the forge.

Peggy waited. When the shoe glowed red hot once more, Bernard lifted it with a pair of tongs and took it to the steel anvil. We stepped further back. Using the curved horn of the anvil, he expertly hammered modifications into the shoe. Sparks flew from the shoe like fireworks. The hammer bounced high after each strike as the anvil returned the energy of the blow. Bernard hammered out his trademark rhythm: bang-bang-a-bang, bang-bang-a-bang; bang-bang, bang-bang, bang-bang.

'Boom Bang-a-bang!' I shouted above the noise.

'Aye. If Lulu had needed an anvil chorus to win Eurovision, then Bernard Vanstone would have been the man for the job,' joked Dad. We all laughed at that, even Bernard. With each blow the anvil rang out. The sound not only filled the shed but also filled your head. It bounced back from the walls of the quarry in sharp echo and it bounced around inside your head, leaving your ears ringing. I blinked with every strike; though I tried, it was impossible not to.

Back into the forge once more and then back to the hoof for a second burn. 'This final burn will ensure a very snug fit between the shoe and the hoof,' commentated Old Mr Vanstone. Satisfied with the result, Bernard plunged the finished shoe into a large tub of cold water. The water sizzled and hissed and a huge cloud of steam rose and spread itself on the underside of the rusty metal roof. While he waited for the shoe to cool, Bernard pulled out a brown raggedy handkerchief from under his apron and wiped his forehead. It was the sweat of exertion, of heat and of steam. His face and arms seemed to be tanned by the glow of the forge.

Peggy waited. The final task was to nail the shoe in place. I knew a bit about shoe nails having earned a dodger for every fistful. They were not like ordinary nails. They were silvery bright with a tapering square head that would fit exactly into the nail wells in the shoe. 'There's a secret in their design,' confided Old Mr Vanstone. 'Their shape means that as they're hammered in, they turn outwards away from the central, sensitive part of the foot and come out through the wall of the hoof. If you go too deep in the centre you can injure the horse – that's called "quicking".'

We stepped forward again to watch the final stages. Holding the nails in his teeth, Bernard beat out his usual staccato as he hammered each in turn through the shoe and into the hoof. This time there was no echo as the hoof, designed to absorb impact, also absorbed the sound of metal hammer on metal shoe. Once the nails were through, he bent over their sharp protruding points with a clincher before smoothing everything off with a rasp. He finished by giving the hoof wall a quick coat of oil with an old paintbrush.

Bernard repeated this process for the second hoof. Throughout all of this activity, Peggy stood patiently, apparently unmoved by all the smoke, steam, heat and hammering. It never ceased to amaze me that, despite everything that went on, horses always seemed to be so relaxed in the hands of the farrier. As the second shoe was finished, Old Mr Vanstone mentioned Danny.

'Eric was saying old Dan is limping,' he informed Bernard.

'Is he? When did he start?'

'George spotted it at the weekend,' replied Dad.

'How was he last time he was in?' Old Mr Vanstone asked Bernard.

'Let's see. Old Dan,' he said to himself. 'I saw him last week, didn't I?' He gave this some thought and then eventually shook his head. 'No,' he concluded, 'I don't recall anything unusual with him last time. It was a straightforward shoeing. Would you like me to come down and have a look at him?' Dad thanked him but said that we had already arranged for the vet to come out. 'Right you are, but if you need a nail pulling just give me a call,' he offered. Dad thanked him again and then they both went into the office to settle up.

I waited in the yard, holding Peggy. 'Don't worry,' assured Old Mr Vanstone, 'the vet will be able to tell if the hoof has been quicked, and if it has, then Bernard will come out to take the shoe off and remove the nail.' Dad came back. We said our farewells and walked Peggy back to the float.

For the homeward journey we always followed Quarry Street to its end, where it crossed the dual carriageway. The traffic lights on Menlove Avenue were back on and there was no sign of the policeman. Peggy trotted on down Woolton Road. As we passed the overgrown field next to Clarke Gardens, I heard the familiar song of a skylark. I could recognise the songs of most of the common birds. I had learnt them from listening to the LP 'A Tapestry of British Bird Song' by Victor C. Lewis, which claimed 'all reproductions achieved without the use of parabolic reflectors'. I had no idea what a parabolic reflector was. Tubs said it was something a cricketer puts down the front of his pants to protect his 'pair-a-bollicks', but I was sure that was wrong because Mum had bought the LP at the church Christmas fair. The skylark performed its trilling song, seemingly without pausing for breath; it flowed continuously, like a mountain stream. Despite this, it was difficult to locate it in the vast sky. After keenly scanning the heavens, I eventually spotted the tiny black dot, hovering and parachuting against the white backdrop of the clouds.

'Skylark!' I announced, pointing at the dot.

'Aye,' acknowledged Dad, but without looking. He had been a bit quiet since we left the smithy.

'Was I wrong to tell Old Mr Vanstone about Danny?' I ventured, after a moment.

'No, no, that's fine,' he replied.

'It's just that, afterwards, I felt like you had maybe wanted, you know, to keep it secret.'

'No. Not a secret. I, well, I wasn't going to mention any-thing just yet because Danny's lameness may have nothing to do with shoeing and I, erm, I didn't want to worry Bernard unnecessarily. But Old Mr Vanstone is probably right. Bernard would want to know.'

'Will he think it's his fault?'

'He probably will, knowing him, but even if it is a quicked hoof it won't be his fault. Every hoof is different and they change over time, so even a master farrier like Bernard can catch a sensitive quick. Danny is getting old and it might be he's developed a weakness in his hoof that he didn't have before. You just never know. A quicked hoof is just one of those things; an occupational hazard. Anyway, let's wait and see what the vet says.'

'Let's hope he makes a "quick" recovery,' I quipped. Dad smiled but he didn't laugh.

Peggy trotted on. Then she did what horses do: she farted. But it wasn't one of those explosive, full-blooded blunder-busses. Rather, it was a series of phut-phut-phut-phut-phuts that were discharged in time with her trot and went on and on. That made Dad laugh.

'Ayyup! There she blows!' he announced. 'That reminds me of a story about the Queen of England,' he went on. 'She had been out driving a horse and carriage, accompanied by a footman, when all of a sudden the horse farted. They both ignored this. It happened a second time. The Queen tutted but said nothing. When it happened a third time, the Queen felt she had to say something rather than face another uncomfortable silence. "I do apologise," she said, "that is so embarrassing." The footman replied, "there's no need to apologise Ma'am, I thought it was the horse!"'

He found this joke so funny that he was only just able to finish telling it. He laughed so much that he started himself coughing. It must have been one of his favourites because I had heard him tell it many times before. It was not particularly funny anymore, but he enjoyed it so much that I did not have the heart to tell him. Besides, the main thing was that the laughter was back. Things were good again.

Peggy trotted on.

Chapter Eight

FOOLS AND HORSES

Six members of the Duke Street Kids stood in the lean-to, next to the walk-in refrigerator. The seventh member, Tubs, was inside the refrigerator. He had previously stayed in there for nineteen minutes and he wanted to see if he could make it to twenty minutes. He had announced this to us wearing his serious face. He said that he had been practising, counting to himself so that he would know when to knock on the door to be let out. He reasoned that if he counted aloud in seconds, then by the time he reached one-thousand-two-hundred, it would be exactly twenty minutes.

We called it 'Fridge Fright'. It was a test of nerve more than a test of physical endurance. To maintain its low temperature, the fridge door created a thermal seal and that meant that no light got in. You could only open the door from the outside and once you were inside and the door was shut, it was so dark that if you held up your hand in front of your face, you could not see it. You lost yourself in there. You lost track of time and of space. Every minute seemed like ten and every ten seemed like an hour.

The darkness and the coldness were like nothing we had ever experienced before. I had said it must be like Jesus' tomb in the Children's Illustrated Bible. But then Trebor had said it must be like being buried alive in a coffin. Now that was really scary. After he'd said that you could not stand in there without thinking about being buried alive. You could not see a thing and all you could hear was the whirring of the motor that kept the fridge going. No adult knew that you were in there, so you were totally dependent on your mates outside.

The game we played was to see who could stay in there the longest. Uncle Robert had a watch with a second hand on it, so he did the timing. The longest I had been in there, before banging on the door to be let out, was twelve minutes. For me, it wasn't just the darkness and the thought of being left in there forever with no way out; it was also the cold. From my earliest memories I had always had a problem with the cold. When the rest of the family were out playing in the snow, I would have to retreat indoors with my poor aching fingers. Now that I was older, it still affected me. It was particularly bad after playing football for the school on Garston Park, in the winter time. It was a blue pain, a paralysing agony for which there was no remedy other than waiting for your blood to finish recirculating into your fingers. There was no way I was able to just grin and bear it. It made me cry every single time it happened and that was so embarrassing. When we finished the match and returned to school I would hide in a toilet cubicle, crying, waiting for the pain to subside. Dad said it was just down to poor circulation.

Uncle Robert kept an eye on his watch; it had just turned two o'clock. He said that the watch was a present from his gran when he had started comprehensive school. Both he and Bonzo went to New Heys Comprehensive School and that's where Falco, Trebor and Shithead were going. Tubs was going to Gateacre Comp and I was going to Quarry Bank Comp (Mum had once had high hopes of me going to a grammar school, but I was crap at grammar). The intake areas for these three schools seemed to converge on Garston, so you could be split up from your mates, depending on which side of a line you lived. To make matters worse, the lines seemed to change each year. We knew of the Gregson family, who all lived in the same house but they had two kids at New Heys and two at Quarry Bank.

I had asked Mum about getting a transfer to New Heys so that I could be with my mates, but she had said no. If I couldn't go to the grammar school, then I was going to go to Quarry Bank because that was where some of my uncles had gone. She tried to make it sound exciting by telling me that John Lennon was a Quarry Banker and that is why his first band with Paul McCartney was called 'The Quarrymen'. I told this to the lads but they were not impressed. They just said that they would rather go to New Heys than be a 'Quarry Wanker'. Well, at least I would not be going to the same school as Steven Scales. He had gone to St John Almond, the catholic comprehensive school.

I had already been into town with Mum to buy my school uniform. Wearing a uniform would be a totally new experience as we didn't have to wear one at primary school. I must admit, I looked pretty smart. Mum had shown me a photo of her brother Ron when he was in the fifth year at Quarry Bank. He also wore a cap and short trousers, so when I tried on my uniform, I looked just like him. 'Decked up like a May horse', Dad had said.

Uncle Robert and Bonzo told us more about what it was like at comprehensive school. It sounded so very different from what we had been used to. They said that there were twenty forms in each year; we only had one form in each year at primary school. Their school day was split into periods: four in the morning and three in the afternoon. In our school you were only taught by one teacher, but they had a different teacher for every subject. Their school had a playing field; ours just had a playground. Every day they were given homework to do; we had never been given homework at primary school. They said that so many kids went to school on bikes that they had long bike sheds to lock them up in.

'Ha! The bike sheds,' snorted Bonzo.

'Whey-hey!' laughed Uncle Robert. 'We can't tell yers what goes on behind the bike sheds though.'

Uncle Robert's 'whey-hey' aroused my curiosity. I had an inkling what that implied. 'Why not?' I demanded.

''Cos yous lot are too young,' said Bonzo. The two of them laughed.

I wanted to press them further but just then Granddad came into the lean-to. He had been in the shippon with Dad and Uncle George seeing a man in a donkey jacket, 'on business'. The donkey jacket had left, but Granddad announced that he was expecting the vet to arrive any minute to look at Danny, so he asked us to leave the yard to give the vet room to work. When he spoke to us, Granddad referred to us as 'young men'. This made us all feel very grown up and even though we wanted to stay in the yard, everyone acceded to Granddad's request without question.

We walked out of the yard just as Bernard Vanstone arrived. He drew up in the oldest, rustiest, most battered old van you could imagine. It looked like he had welded it together using assorted bits of scrap metal from the smithy. I remembered how he had offered to come out if Danny needed to have a shoe removed. He parked outside the gates and went into the yard where Dad, Granddad and Uncle George were waiting.

We walked down Duke Street. Because it ran down the slope of Garston, the houses on Duke Street had different levels of front doorsteps to cope with the gradient. The group of houses at the top of the street had no front step; the next few had a small step; the next few, a large step; the next few, a large and a small step; and, finally those at the bottom of the street had two large steps. Falco's house had two large steps, which meant that there was room for us all to sit down together.

I was explaining to the lads that Danny was going a bit lame and that was the reason why vet was coming out, when a car turned into the top of Duke Street and then turned again, into the stable yard. I said that it must be the vet and that I'd catch up with them later. I legged it back to the yard just in time to see the vet pulling his bag from the back seat of his car.

Our vet was Mr Tomlinson. He was a short ginger-haired man with a nose like the beak of a golden eagle. Dad, Uncle George, Granddad and Bernard were all waiting in the doorway to Danny's stable. Mr Tomlinson went over and shook hands with them all. I hovered in the background.

I was still wary of Bernard. When they all went into Danny's stable, I waited at the stable door.

The vet unslung his shoulder bag and placed it in the corner of the stable. He then 'introduced' himself to Danny by talking to him while he patted him and placed his hand under his muzzle. I knew that this would put the horse at ease by letting him experience the touch, sound and smell of the newcomer. Mr Tomlinson then moved around Danny, bending down to inspect each hoof in turn but all the time keeping one hand in contact with the horse, patting his neck, flank or hindquarters. While he was doing this, Dad told the vet when the problem had first been noticed and described what had happened since then.

'How old is he?' Mr Tomlinson began to look into Danny's mouth.

'Twenty-eight years, nine months and thirteen days,' replied Dad without hesitation and with a straight face; everyone else smiled.

'I see,' said the vet as he decided to forgo examining Danny's teeth. He then declared that he wanted to see Danny walking, so we all filed out into the street. Uncle George walked Danny halfway down Duke Street and back again.

'Once more please, Mr Joy, and just trot him back to me,' instructed Mr Tomlinson, who was now clearly in charge of the situation. Uncle George obliged while Mr Tomlinson bent forward with his hands on his knees and watched carefully. We regrouped around Danny, back in the yard.

'Okay,' began Mr Tomlinson. 'It's as you thought. He's lame in his nearside fore and it looks like the problem is in the foot rather than in the leg. If it is quicked, there will be a build-up of pus as the body fights any infection. It's the build-up of pus that will be putting pressure on the quick of the hoof and that will cause lameness. Let's have a closer look, shall we?'

While Uncle George held Danny, Mr Tomlinson inspected the hoof. He scraped away at the underside with a knife he produced from a pocket in his jacket. 'Aye,' he confirmed to himself and then he asked Bernard to remove the shoe. Bernard unclinched the nails, lifted the shoe and then pulled each nail, handing them to the vet as he did so. Mr Tomlinson held up the fifth nail and showed us the traces of blood and pus on it.

'That's the one,' he announced.

'Damn,' swore Bernard.

'Not your fault, my friend,' declared the vet. 'He's an old horse so goodness knows what is going on with his quick and 'smiths don't come with X-ray vision. I know you're good, Bernard, but no 'smith is that good.'

I asked if the pus would come out now that the nail had been pulled. Mr Tomlinson turned and looked at me as if he had noticed me for the first time. 'That's an interesting question, young man,' he smiled. I glowed. 'Well, actually, it depends.' He turned back to the men. 'Sometimes that's all it takes but if it's formed an abscess the hoof will stay hot until the abscess bursts. That could take a while, but there may be a way of doing things a bit quicker. Let's have another look, shall we?'

He picked up the now shoeless hoof once more and resumed scraping with his knife. There was a dark spot in the general whiteness of the sole. Using the handle of the knife, he tapped the spot to see if the horse would flinch. He must have felt something because he then concentrated his scraping on that spot. As he worked, he asked when Danny had last received an anti-tetanus injection. Dad told him that it would have been in June 1963. He continued scraping. Eventually, pus popped out under pressure and formed a yellowy-green bubble on the surface of the hoof. 'Ah, that should do it,' he said with satisfaction. It might have been my imagination but I could have sworn I heard Danny give a sigh and visibly relax in the hands of the vet as the pressure was released.

Mr Tomlinson wiped away the pus with a cloth that appeared from another pocket of his jacket. He then waited to see if more would come to the surface. Eventually, he turned to me. 'Would you be kind enough to fetch me my bag, young man?' I glowed again and quickly retrieved his bag from the corner of the stable and brought it back out into the yard, where I set it down beside him.

He placed the hoof back on the ground and went rummaging through his bag. 'Right,' he decided, taking the necessary equipment from his bag. 'I'm going to treat the wound with iodine and then I'll give him an anti-tetanus jab.' We watched as he carried out this treatment.

When he had finished, he addressed his attentive audience. 'I'm still a bit concerned,' he admitted. 'There was only a fraction of the amount of pus I was expecting. It could be that there is an abscess higher up the hoof. If that's the case then we will have to wait for it to rise up the foot and burst at the coronet.'

'Hmmm,' Bernard nodded his head in agreement. 'What do you recommend, then?'

'I suggest we leave him as he is for now and let the iodine do its job. It should harden up the hoof near the injury and help to seal it. I'll call back tomorrow. If there is no abscess, he should be walking better by then. In the meantime, you need to keep the hoof clean.'

'I've brought a boot with me just in case,' offered Bernard. He went to his van and came back with a leather hoof boot, that we could strap on to Danny's hoof to protect it while it was without a shoe. The boot would also keep the hoof clean.

Dad thanked Mr Tomlinson and he got back in his van and went on his way. Bernard helped Uncle George to put the boot on to Danny's hoof. 'Let me have it back whenever you're ready,' he told Dad. 'There's no hurry.' Then everyone thanked Bernard. As he was leaving he came over to me and ruffled my hair. 'Here's a souvenir for you, meladdo.' I held out my hand and into my palm he dropped the nail that had quicked the hoof. He left the yard, climbed into his van and set off back to the smithy.

Holding the nail, I walked back down Duke Street to find the lads. They were still sitting on Falco's steps. I showed them the nail and told them what the vet had found. I described to them how he had drained the pus from the hoof.

'We was wondering why it was taking so long,' said Bonzo. 'We thought the vet might be having to put the horse down or summit.'

'No. Nuffin like that,' I assured them. 'Why? What time is it now then?'

Uncle Robert glanced down at his watch. Then suddenly, he cried out, with genuine alarm, 'Fugginell!' He put his hands to his head and looked at us with horror in his eyes. 'TUBS! He's been in the fridge for a fuggin hour!'

Shee-it! I couldn't believe that we had forgotten about Tubs. He had only wanted to stay in for twenty minutes. We all legged it back up Duke Street towards the stable yard. My mind raced as fast as my legs. I feared to think what we might find when we opened the door. No one had stayed in there for an hour. Would he be okay? Would he be a gibbering, frightened wreck? Flippin' eck! Would he be frozen stiff? Surely not. Surely all of that blubber he carried would protect him like it did the seals in the Arctic. What would I tell Dad if Tubs was frozen to death? Could we get away with just leaving him in there until Dad went to the fridge to get the milk out in the morning? Hang on a minute, I thought, the milk was not frozen, it was just cold. Surely then, Tubs would still be alive. Wouldn't he?

I was the fastest, so I turned into the stable yard first. To my relief there was no sign of the adults. I ran into the lean-to with the rest of the gang on my heels. I stopped in front of the fridge and turned to look at the others, hoping someone would step forward to open the door. I could see it in their faces — we were all expecting the worst.

'Go 'ed, Deejay,' prompted Bonzo.

I pulled the levered handle and there was a loud click as it unlocked. I pulled again at the heavy door and it slowly swung open. Tubs was standing there, hunched over and shivering. He put his hand to his forehead to shade his eyes from the daylight. He squinted at us and tried to pucker out his lips to make himself look important, but his chattering teeth spoiled the effect. He whispered: 'th-th-three th-th-thousand, s-s-six h-h-hundred-d-d an' t-t-two.'

Chapter Nine

SALT OF THE EARTH

The following day the vet returned. He arrived not long after lunch. This time there was just myself, Dad and Uncle George to meet him. Uncle George walked Danny up and down Duke Street again while Mr Tomlinson looked on.

'I'm not happy with that,' he declared, shaking his head. 'He's still lame.' We walked Danny back to his stable. 'I reckon there's still infection in there and we need to drive it out. So, the best thing to do is to soak the hoof each day in a bucket of Epsom salt. That'll drive any abscess up to the coronet, where it'll come out.' He had a tin of salt with him, which he handed to Dad and then told him how it should be administered. 'Do that each day for the next week,' he advised, 'and I'll come back to see him then. In the meantime take him for a walk around the block every other day just to stave off any problems with the other hooves and to make sure he doesn't stiffen up.'

Dad thanked Mr Tomlinson again and we waved him off. Uncle George fetched a plastic bucket from the shippon and then took it to get some warm water from the house. While he was gone, Mum arrived with Ann and Billy. They came and found us in the stable yard. I was not expecting them and I presumed that Mum had some business at church or was going to go shopping in the village. But, to my surprise, she pulled from her bag the family's Box Brownie 127 camera and announced it had a new film in it and was all ready to go.

'Right!' announced Dad. 'I'll just go and get George,' and off he went.

I asked Mum what was happening. She explained that Dad wanted to take some photographs of the horses. 'But, what for?' I persisted.

'Because we don't have any, that's what for,' she retorted.

Thinking about this, I concluded that she was right. We had lots of photographs of us growing up, usually on holiday in Blackpool, but in all of those albums there was not a single photograph of life at the dairy. The only photograph I had ever seen of any of the horses was the one that hung up in the cold room next to a lime green certificate. It was a picture of Dad driving Rupert at the Liverpool Show. The certificate announced that we had come third in the Tradesman's Class. On that day Ann had been allowed to ride in the milk float – 'you're too young, besides there's only room for one passenger,' I had been told by Mum. I so wished I had been born first.

Dad returned with Uncle George. They went into the shippon and brought out Rupert and Peggy. The sun was shining onto the side of the Duke of Wellington Hotel and the painted cream walls reflected it back warmly. Mum decided that the hotel would make a better photographic backdrop than the dark and grimy redbrick walls of the shippon.

'Black horses against a dirty background won't work', she pointed out when Dad questioned this. 'Besides, if those black horses are being held in front of a dirty background by a dirty old man, all you'll see on the photo will be a ruddy pair of white ears.'

'I'm not old,' laughed Dad.

He led Rupert into Duke Street followed by Uncle George, leading Peggy. They posed in front of the hotel while Mum stood with her back to the dairy. She held the Box Brownie against her chest, cradled in the palm of her left hand. She then looked down into the viewfinder, shading it with her right hand to prevent any reflection. She had to move her whole body to get everything in frame. She did this for each shot, eventually announcing 'Say cheese!' before pressing down the lever with her right thumb. She was well practiced at using the Box Brownie, but each photo seemed to take forever.

By this time, Nana and Granddad had come out to watch from the dairy door. Uncle George then held both horses while Dad went back into the stable yard to fetch Danny. Granddad and Uncle George then posed with all three horses for another couple of shots.

'Right, let's have a few with the children now,' decided Mum.

Ann asked if we could have them taken with Danny, so Uncle George led Rupert and Peggy back into the shippon. We posed with Danny. Ann stood next to the horse, holding the reins, with Billy next to her. I was standing at the back and I was not too pleased about this. Ann was always the first, no matter what we did. Then I had a brainwave.

'Can I get on his back?' I asked Dad.

'No, he's lame', interjected Ann.

But Dad said 'Aye, why not,' and tossed me up on to Danny's back. The cheeky grin I'm wearing in that photograph says it all – look at me, at last, I'm on top. Yessss!

When Mum had finished off the reel, Dad announced, 'Right, while I've got him out I may as well take him 'round the block for a bit of exercise'. I asked if I could stay on his back. 'Aye, I suppose so. You're too light to make any difference to Danny.' Yes! Another victory.

We set off down Duke Street, Dad leading Danny with me perched on his back and Ann and Billy walking on the pavement. And as we did so, something unusual happened. Although the people who lived in the streets near to the dairy must have been used to the comings and goings of the horses, for some reason they came out of their houses to see me riding Danny.

Maybe it was just the sight of a horse out of harness, not between the shafts, or maybe the kids thought that Dad was giving rides to everybody. Whatever the reason, as we passed by, people stood at their front doors to watch and the kids from each house came out to follow us; everyone had big smiles on their faces. By the time we turned left into James Street we had about a dozen kids walking along at the side and behind the horse. It was great! I felt like the Pied Piper and Hannibal all rolled into one. The kids packed the narrow pavement on Danny's nearside and flowed along like the wash from a passing Mersey ferry.

We turned left into Chapel Road and passed Caulfield's pet shop on the corner. In its window I could see the large cage containing the mynah bird. It was an excellent pet shop – more like a mini zoo – and it smelled of wood shavings. If any of the Duke Street Kids had a jar of tadpoles at home we would all go to Caulfield's to buy a tub of ants' eggs to feed to them; but that was just a convenient excuse to go in and spend time looking at all the animals.

As well as the usual rabbits, hamsters, guinea pigs and budgerigars, they had terrapins, African toads, tree frogs, coldwater fish, tropical fish, canaries, zebra finches, chameleons, praying mantis and just occasionally, a capuchin monkey. We would spend half an hour in there before Mrs Caulfield would tell us to either buy something or leave the shop. One of us would purchase the tub of ants' eggs and that would buy us another ten minutes as we slowly exited the shop. All this time, Shithead would be standing next to the mynah bird's cage, whispering to it – trying to teach it to say 'Shit!' It had been great fun, but we were all too old now for that sort of stuff.

The entourage grew as older kids brought out their younger brothers and sisters to join the parade, holding them by the hand. Some walked next to Dad asking him questions. Others walked at the side, enviously looking up at me, whilst others followed just behind. It was like the picture of Palm Sunday in the Children's Illustrated Bible. More adults came to their front doors to see the spectacle. They laughed at the sight of all the children following the horse and they waved to me. It was great being the centre of all this attention.

Dad answered all questions with his usual good humour. They came thick and fast in a never-ending stream of curiosity:

'Where are yer takin' 'im?'

'Why issee wearin' a boot on one futt?'

'Wot's wrong wivvim?'

'Wotsisname?'

''Owoldizzy?'

'Can I 'avva ride?'

'Dus'ee bite?'

'Izzey wild?'

'Can I take 'im 'ome wivvme?'

I looked ahead and coming towards us was a car I recognised. This could be perfect. I looked intently at the oncoming vehicle, trying to identify the occupants. I straightened my back and squared my shoulders to look as tall as possible. The car slowed down as it approached us. The woman driving it was telling her children in the back to look at the horse. As it passed I could clearly see who was sitting on the back seat, looking out from behind the car window – it was the girl from the launderette. I looked straight into her eyes. She looked straight back at me and then, with a lovely smiling face, she waved. I raised my arm and gave a full wave back. I watched her over my shoulder as the car drove on. I felt ten feet tall; like John Wayne, like Buffalo Bill, like the Lone Ranger, like Richard the Lionheart, like Robin Hood, like Ivanhoe, like, like – like D'Artagnan! This was a magic moment.

Then I felt what I thought was something biting my calf. I looked down to see Steven Scales grinning back up at me. He had pinched my leg. No one else seemed to have noticed. Dad was too busy talking to the children next to him. I looked around for any of the Duke Street Kids, but there were none to be seen. I pulled my leg higher up Danny's back, out of Scales' reach. The magic evaporated. From being the King of the Castle, suddenly, I came tumbling down, like the Dirty Rascal. I felt very exposed and vulnerable. My earlier pride was about to take another knock.

The walk was not only exercising Danny's leg and back muscles but also his bowel muscles. He raised his tail and let rip. 'Phwaaarrrr!' someone shouted, ''ees just farted!' Then Danny followed through and dumped his load in the road. The kids went mad with feigned disgust. A big 'Urrrrrrgh!' went up from the rear and someone else shouted, 'Mr Joy! Yer 'orse is shittin'!' There were more rude finger-pointing hysterics. It felt like they were laughing at me. I found it difficult to maintain my smile and I was starting to feel embarrassed.

I looked to Dad for some relief from my plight and he did not fail me. He turned and looked back at me and laughed his way through: 'Oh Danny Boy, the pipes, the pipes are calling.' That made me feel better. When you are laughing at yourself, no one can laugh at you – only with you.

An old man ran out from one of the terraced houses. He was carrying a bucket and hand shovel. 'Thank you very much, Eck,' he called to Dad. 'That'll go nicely on me rhubarb.' As he began scraping the muck off the road, some of the kids broke away to see what he was doing. Scales went with them. That made me feel even better.

'What's ee doin'?' someone asked aloud.

'Ee's gonna put shit on 'is rhubarb,' someone else answered.

'I prefer to put custard on mine,' laughed Dad.

There was a moment's pause while that one sunk in and then, together, everyone groaned 'Urghhhhhhhh!' Then we all laughed.

As we walked on we passed Ali Slavin's barber shop with its smell of aftershave and red and white striped pole mounted outside. Of course, his name wasn't really Ali. It was just that we called all barbers 'Ali' after Ali Baba. Slavin's was where

I would go with Dad to get a 'short-back-n-sides', finished off with Brylcreem. Then you had to run the gauntlet of the Duke Street Kids getting 'first wet'. This involved them spitting on their hand and slapping you on your head, the first one to do so shouting 'first wet!' We had no idea why we did this or what significance it had, but we always did it to whichever one of us had had a haircut. I usually went to Slavin's about every six weeks but it was now nearer eight weeks since my last visit. I had not mentioned this to Mum or Dad as I was hoping to let it grow long – like a Beatles haircut.

Next door to Slavin's was Bob's Ice Cream and it smelled of, well, ice cream. Bob made his ice cream with milk bought from Wellington Dairy. Dad said Bob was a very good customer. As well as the shop he had an ice cream van, which would patrol the streets where we lived, off Garston Old Road. Bob made his ice cream in the traditional way; it was stiff ice cream served using a scoop. He used to be the only van around but then another van appeared selling Mr Whippy ice cream, a new soft ice cream that came out of a machine. Mum always insisted we bought Bob's ice cream because he bought our milk, but we liked Mr Whippy. When we heard the van's music playing we'd leg it outside to see if it was Bob or Mr Whippy and we'd always tell Mum it was Bob. She would give us the money for a cone each. If we bought a Mr Whippy we had to make sure we ate it before Mum saw it. Eventually she caught us out – she had a dickey fit.

We turned into Wellington Street. Standing on the corner was Toxteth Technical School, otherwise known as the 'Tocky-Tech' or the 'Tick-Tock'. Its tall red-brick walls were surrounded by railings, which we used to climb over to play football in the playground. When the cocky watchman came, we would leg it shouting: 'It's the Ticky-Tocky-Cocky!' In all that time he never caught us – but we were too old now for that sort of stuff.

As we passed the end of Wood Street we approached the fish and chip shop, which, like every fish and chip shop in the entire city of Liverpool, was referred to by everyone as 'the chippy'. All the kids called the owner of this chippy 'Mr Chips'. Whenever Dad was leaving the shop he would say 'Goodbye – Mr Chips', and then laugh through his teeth at his own joke. The aroma from there always made you feel hungry, even if you had just eaten your dinner. During term-time dinner hours, the shop was packed with the students from the Tick-Tock. Dad said the shop survived on the money the students spent there. Next to the chippy was Hilda's, a general store.

Nana bought her bread there, Granddad bought his matches there and Dad bought his boot polish there. But, to us kids, Hilda's was a sweet shop – and what a sweet shop it was. Inside, its shelved walls were lined with jars containing every sort of sweet imaginable, sold by the quarter or half pound. But our favourites were behind the glass counter. For one penny you could buy any four sweets from liquorice-flavoured Blackjacks, spearmint-flavoured Mojos, to citrus-flavoured Fruit Salads. There were also sherbet dips, Bags-O-Gold chewing gum, flying saucers, red liquorice shoelaces, gobstoppers, white mice, banana chews, Spanish tobacco, chocolate logs, cinder toffee, Bazooka Joe American gum and jelly snakes. In summer Hilda would put pyramidal cartons of orange juice in her freezer and sell them as 'Jublee Icebergs'. Granddad would usually give us a thrupenny dodger each to spend at Hilda's. It was so difficult to choose. You could have a selection of sweets or you could buy one packet of crisps. If I bought crisps I would suck them to make them last as long as possible.

Dad knew all of the traders on the block and they all knew him. He said that they were all good, honest, hard-working people and I suspected that was also what they said about him. They bought their milk from us and, whether it was for ants' eggs, a haircut, ice cream, fish and chips or a bar of Fry's Chocolate Cream, we spent our money with them. Granddad had said that it was the same money that kept going around the block and that was how everyone kept everyone else in business.

He once told me a story about a thrupenny dodger he had just given me to spend at Hilda's. He said that he had got it from Mr Caulfield, who had bought a pint of milk from us; Mr Caulfield had got it from Mr Slavin, who had bought a packet of dog biscuits; Mr Slavin had got it from Bob, who went next door for a shave; Bob had got it from Mr Chips, who had bought a block of ice cream; Mr Chips had got it from Hilda, who had bought a fishcake for her tea; Hilda had got it from me when I had last bought a packet of smoky bacon crisps; and I had got it from Granddad. It made me wonder where the dodger had come from in the first place.

As we turned back into Duke Street there were Falco, Trebor, Shithead and Tubs, waiting outside the gates to the stable yard. We pulled up and Dad lifted me down. As soon as I was down, all the kids seemed to lose interest and they all wandered off. I joined my friends.

'Yer big pozer,' laughed Tubs.

'I know,' I laughed back. 'it was great!' I felt quite comfortable admitting this to the lads. We all liked to show off when we could, but as long as we could laugh about it, we kept each other's feet on the ground. I told them what had happened on the way round but, even though they were my trusted friends, I did not say anything about the girl in the launderette. I told them about Scales.

'He's just been in trouble with the bizzies again,' reported Falco. 'They've had him in at Heald Street.'

'Yeah,' agreed Tubs, looking important, 'me old fella says he's been arsin'.' There was a moment's silence – then I asked him what his dad meant by that. 'Erm, I suppose he means arsin' around with fire,' offered Tubs, looking a bit less important.

'No, yer plant pot!' Trebor chided. 'He meant 'arson' – setting fire to stuff.' He turned to me to explain. 'Scales burnt down the scout hut. We've just been up Kettle Nook to have a look at it. It's knackered. They're going to have to build another one.'

'Is he going to be arrested?' I asked with a hint of optimism.

'Nah. He's been boasting about it, but the scuffers can't prove anything,' replied Shithead.

'He's just a nasty piece of work,' concluded Tubs with recovered importance, pursing his lips and shaking his head like an adult would do. We all agreed.

The five of us stepped into the stable yard to allow Dad to close the gates behind us. We ambled over to Danny's stable. Uncle George had a bucket of warm water ready with the salt dissolved in it. Dad went into the stable to hold Danny while Uncle George took the boot off the hoof and placed the injured foot into the bucket. Ann and Billy stood in the corner of the stable and looked on. Me and the lads watched over the stable half door.

'What's in the bucket?' Falco asked.

'Salt,' replied Dad.

'What? Like salt 'n' vinegar?' Tubs said. We all laughed.

Dad explained that it was a special salt called Epsom salt, which had been dissolved in the water. He said that Epsom salt had all sorts of medicinal uses but it was particularly good for reducing swelling.

Tubs thought about this. 'It can't be that good,' he stated.

'Oh,' Dad snorted. 'And why not?'

'Well,' explained Tubs, wearing his best serious face. 'Me ma puts Epsom salt in her bath and even though she stays in there for hours, it hasn't reduced her swelling one jot.'

That made Dad laugh. 'In that case, let's hope Danny has better luck than your ma,' he replied, still laughing.

'Aye,' agreed Uncle George. He wasn't laughing.

Chapter Ten

UNDER THE BRIDGE

In the second week of the summer holidays I slept over at the dairy, using the spare bedroom at the back of the house. Dad had already been up and about for a while when he came to wake me in time to do the bottom round.

The business had two milk rounds: an early morning 'under the bridge' round and a mid-morning 'over the bridge' round ('bottom round' and 'top round', respectively). It was impossible to find a route in or out of this part of Garston without passing under or over a railway bridge of some description. 'Under the bridge' referred to an area in the south of the district of Garston. At the bottom of the village were the traffic lights that marked the junction of St Mary's Road and Church Road. The railway that served the docks ran over Church Road Bridge, and this marked the entrance to that part of Garston which, in typical Garstonian logic, was referred to by everyone as 'under the bridge'. The bridge was the gateway to Garston's south docks and to the numerous industrial 'werks' that the port had spawned. Generations of

Garstonians had worked in the 'bobbinwerks', the 'match-werks', the 'gaswerks', the 'levverwerks' or the 'botullwerks'.

It was only the excitement of doing the rounds that persuaded me to leave the depth and warmth of the feather mattress and blankets. As I was dressing I could hear the intermittent disgruntled belching of foghorns on the Mersey. I pulled back the curtains to reveal what was troubling the river traffic: it was a misty morning. I pushed up the sash window and breathed in the moist air. It was cool and it left a taste of tin on the back of my throat. I wondered if Dad would have to light the candles in the van's brass coach lamps, like he did during the winter. But then I dismissed the idea. I was confident the sun would soon burn off the mist.

I pulled down the window, went downstairs and then ran a quick relay race to the toilet at the bottom of the yard. At Garston Old Road we had an inside toilet in the bathroom, but Nana and Granddad had never felt the need to have one fitted. Dad was always making jokes about the outside lavvy. It was located at the furthest edge of the property, away from the house. Dad said that this was to 'keep the hum away from the home'. But it had the disadvantage of exposing you to the elements in order to get there. At night time the challenge was doubled, in that the toilet did not have the benefit of an electricity supply, so you had to take a lit candle with you. This was not easy if it was blowing a gale or chucking it down. Once inside the toilet you placed the candle on a ledge provided especially for that purpose. Dad said it beggared belief that the combination of naked flame and methane gas in such a confined space did not have explosive consequences. It may well have been primitive but it was clinically clean. The walls were whitewashed, the floor tiles gleamed and the polished wood of the toilet seat really did shine. 'You could eat your dinner off of that toilet seat,' Dad would say. 'If you were so inclined, that is,' he would add, and then laugh through his teeth, enjoying his own wit.

How long you spent in there not only depended on what you had to do, but also on the time of the week. The whole family business was run on an environmentalist basis, in that you made best use of whatever resources were at hand. Well, in the toilet, what was at hand was the *Radio Times*. Granddad was either the ultimate recycler or the ultimate miserable old bugger. Every Friday night, the out-of-date edition of the *Radio Times* was unstapled and cut into quarters using a bread knife. One corner of this wad was then holed using a penknife and threaded with a loop of baling string. The wad was then hung on a nail in the toilet wall and that was your toilet paper. The magazine was made up of colourful glossy pages on which the adverts were printed and soft matt pages on which the radio and television schedules were printed. Even though you could end up with Monday night's schedule printed backwards on your cheeks if you used the soft pages, if you had a choice you would always use them first. Consequently, by the end of the week, you were left with only the glossy pages. These had a quality that was the direct opposite of absorbent and using them could be a long and distinctly uncomfortable ordeal.

On this occasion there were four of the soft pages left on the otherwise glossy wad. I used two and pocketed the other two in case I needed to go again later in the day. I raced back into the kitchen to wash my hands and face in water that was as cold as a snowman's handshake. The sharpness of the water was guaranteed to shatter any remnant of sleepiness. I wolfed down a piece of syrup-laden toast that Nana had waiting for me on the kitchen dresser and then ran back down the whitewashed passageway to the stable yard.

By the time I arrived, Dad and Uncle George had already taken the crates of milk out of the walk-in refrigerator and loaded them into the back of the van. Uncle George was backing Rupert between the shafts. This operation was a daily routine for horse and driver and it was completed with the bare minimum of verbal instruction from the latter. The harness was of the collar and hames design. It was all polished brass and oiled leather. Dad would spend hours polishing and oiling it. I knew how it all worked. The thick leather collar allowed the horse to use his muscular shoulders to pull the van. The hames (brass rings) on the collar were attached to chain traces, which were in turn attached to cleats on the base of the shafts. Around the horse's haunches was the leather breeching. This was attached to cleats near the front of the shafts by two breeching straps. The breeching allowed the horse to hold back the van when going downhill. Dad would say that the collar was the gas, the breeching was the brake and the hay was the petrol. He also had something to say about the exhaust.

While Uncle George hitched Rupert to the van, I looked in on Danny. The abscess in his hoof had burst, but he wasn't yet fit to return to work. Then, Dad opened the gates to the yard and stood in the street to ensure there was no traffic coming. I stepped up into the van and Uncle George passed the reins to me through the front window. He removed the wheel chock, climbed aboard and took the reins back from me. He then gave two clicks out of the corner of his mouth. In response, Rupert leaned into his collar, walked on and drew us out of the yard. We never closed the gates behind us when the van was out, even though the yard was unattended. Dad stood to attention and saluted us with a big grin on his face and then as the van swung round to go down Duke Street, he jumped aboard and we were under way at walking pace.

At seven o'clock in the morning the traffic on St Mary's Road was not too heavy, so at the bottom of Duke Street we turned right on to James Street and then left on to the high street. This brought us out very close to the traffic lights at the bottom of the village. Rupert would walk this short stretch with the breeching straps taut as he held back the weight of the fully laden van against the slope of the village. At the lights, the slope bottomed out. The breeching straps relaxed and the strain was taken up by the traces, which tightened as we turned right to go 'under the bridge'. Two clicks of the tongue and a shake of the reins from Uncle George and Rupert broke into a steady trot.

On our left we passed St Michael's church, with its large sandstone-walled embankment. At the bottom of the grave-yard, Church Road turned ninety degrees to the left and became Banks Road. As we turned the corner, a flash of grey and black swooped from the graveyard, flew low over the van and headed off towards the railway sidings in Kings Street.

I recognised that shape and the striped chest immediately. 'Sparrowhawk! Female!' I cried, pointing at the rapidly diminishing object.

'Was it?' Dad said, squinting into the distance. 'That'll be what's been nesting in the bell tower. It's made a hell of a mess of the church porch.'

'Really?'

'Yes. Even the vicar calls it a "Shithawk".' I made a mental note of that – the nest, not the vicar.

The mist was a bit thicker here, down by the river, and as Rupert's exertions warmed him up he puffed out clouds of moisture from his nostrils. We followed Banks Road past the 'gaswerks' and the 'timba-yard' and then, just before the airport, we turned into Windfield Road. We pulled up in the middle of the road and the two adults dismounted to begin their delivery.

Neither Dad nor Uncle George ever used a written list of customers. They both knew from memory who lived where and what their daily order was. If a customer wanted to change their order on a particular day, they left a note in one of their empties. So, we always carried slightly more milk than had been ordered. The milk came in two sorts: 'sterrie' (sterilised) and 'pasttie' (pasturised). Dad said that when you worked on the round, milk would always be moving 'past-your-eyes'. Bottles of sterrie came with long necks and a metal cap that you could only remove with a bottle opener. Bottles of pasttie were your common milk bottles with the silver foil tops, which blue-tits would peck through to drink the cream; they came in pint and half-pint sizes. We also carried pints and half-pints of orange juice. This was the most gorgeous orange juice I had ever tasted. It was not too bitter like fresh orange juice and not too sweet like cordial orange juice – it was just right. So smooth, it slid down your throat and tantalised your taste buds on the way, leaving a most refreshing aftertaste in your mouth. It was a delightful way to quench your thirst on a hot day, especially if it was still cold from the walk-in refrigerator.

Dad said it was nectar from the gods, although the bottles said it was orange juice from Hanson's.

Dad loaded up his hand crate and started on the opposite side of the road from Uncle George. However, this was a three-man team and Rupert was the third man. Together, they worked the round in perfect synchronisation. Dad and Uncle George would each have a metal hand crate that carried a dozen bottles. They would load up at the van and then walk off on each side of the road, delivering milk to the doorstep and collecting the empties. When the hand crate was filled with empties they would return to the van, transfer their empties into the crates in the back of the van and top up their hand crate again with the right mix of bottles to serve the next set of houses. But they did not have to drive the horse while they were delivering. As they worked their way along the two rows of houses, either one of them would give Rupert a call: 'Come on!' Rupert would walk the van along the road, catch up with them and then stop. He did this with no one at the reins and he even manoeuvred the van around parked vehicles. 'Can't get a motor to do that,' Uncle George would boast. Rupert never once had an accident doing this; spot-on judgement every time – that's horse sense for you.

Dad said that all Irish Vanners were very intelligent. Rupert knew the meaning of key commands and he could respond to simple questions with a nod or shake of his head. On one occasion, doing the bottom round, Dad had called Rupert on and after taking one step, the horse stopped. Dad called him again but Rupert just stood in the middle of the road and shook his head. When Dad went back to get him he found that a cleat had broken and one of the traces was trailing on the ground. Rupert had either felt or heard the difference and knew there was something wrong. 'You can't get a motor to do that.'

Even though the route had lots of twists and turns, Rupert knew it like the inside of his blinkers and he would execute every turn perfectly. According to Dad, Rupert could take corners better than Stanley Matthews. He also knew where the best grass verges were so he could grab a bite on his way round. His favourite was the square green in Monkfield Way and he would often pull the van on to the green to get to the sweetest grass. Occasionally, a customer would come out and feed him sugar lumps. Uncle George did not approve of that, but he did not say anything to them; he just called 'Come on' to Rupert. The customers soon got out of the way when the van began to move.

I split my time between walking with Dad and staying on board the van to sort the empties. Our last delivery was in Banks Lane, right next to the airport. Sometimes we would see planes landing or taking off over the River Mersey. As Dad and Uncle George climbed back into the van for the last time, I knew that there was a half-pint of orange juice that remained undelivered. I had been watching it for the past hour. I asked Dad if I could drink it.

'Aye, I suppose so,' he acceded. 'You've been good sorting out the empties for us, so an orange juice is probably a fair day's pay. Pass it here.' I duly did so. He ripped off the foil top. It was silver with tiny pictures of round oranges with green leaves on it. He took a quick swig himself and as he wiped his mouth on his sleeve he declared, 'Ah! Nectar from the gods!'

He passed it back to me. He didn't offer it to Uncle George. Every morning, Uncle George drank a glass of milk with a raw egg in it; he didn't drink orange juice. I accepted the bottle and took a long draught. 'Ah!' I declared, mimicking Dad and wiping my mouth on my sleeve. 'Nectar from Hanson's!' Dad laughed at that. I liked making adults laugh, it made me feel special.

A slap of the reins on his rump was the signal to Rupert to begin the return journey. He had completed his two-hour milk round and he was going home. Back to his cosy stall, back to his stable companion, back to a cool spring and some treacle-sweetened hay. The milk had been delivered and the crates were now filled with empties. With a lightened load Rupert pulled the van along effortlessly, with only the barest tension in the traces.

As we had a clear road before us, Uncle George gave the horse his head and with two clicks urged him on. Rupert had no need of encouragement and he stepped out in style. His knees bounced high and the feather on each leg shook across his hooves like four fab Beatle mop-top haircuts. His metal shoes pounded out a rapid staccato as he moved up a gear into a quick trot. This is what he was bred for; an Irish Vanner, in his element. He carried this Vanner legacy in his genes. He was not a thoroughbred, he was a common working horse – the lowest of the low in the equine pecking order. But he wore this badge with pride and with dignity and celebrated his inheritance every weekday morning, as regular as clockwork, delivering the milk.

By now the sun had seen off the last of the mist and it was shining all the way down Banks Road. Its heat rekindled the fresh smell of newly mown grass that wafted from the airport. On board the milk van, we were enjoying the moment as horse and vehicle sailed along, taking the home-ward journey at a cracking clip. I sat on the milk crates at the back of the van. The empty bottles rattled rhythmically in their crates and jumped in unison whenever we ran over a bump in the road. Dad and Uncle George were standing in the front of the van with their backs to me.

'Ayup!' Dad called. 'He thinks he's a ruddy trotter!'

'Aye. One sugar lump too many this morning,' replied Uncle George.

As we approached the ninety-degree turn where Banks Road becomes Church Road, there was not the usual slowing of Rupert's gait. He was obviously feeling energetic enough to take the bend at full tilt. As we swung around, the van began to lean to the left. Dad stepped into the right-hand doorway and leaned out, as if his slight weight could counter the centrifugal force.

'Whoe-ho!' he laughed. 'A bit of the ol' Douglas Fairbanks. Hold tight, Dave.'

I gripped my milk crate seat with both hands and leaned into the bend. Uncle George, with a rein in each hand, stood solid, as if his clogs were nailed to the wooden floor of the van.

Rupert completed the manoeuvre without breaking stride. I stood up to get a better view, moved over to the left and stuck my head out of the open side of the van. The wind hit my face; we were really bombing along.

We passed the church once more and then plunged into the shadow of the railway bridge. The timbre of the hooves changed as the sound echoed back off the sandstone walls and metal underbelly of the bridge. Suddenly, the hoof beats were drowned by the thunder of a goods train rumbling overhead and amplified in the confined space beneath the bridge; an iron horse of the twentieth century above, a work horse of the nineteenth century below. For a moment Rupert was startled into a few strides at canter and the van lurched forward. But his Irish Vanner temperament cooled any panic and directed the new energy into an even faster trot.

We shot out from under the bridge into the sunlight once more. Directly ahead lay the traffic lights at the bottom of the village. They were on green and there was no traffic ahead of us, so Rupert had an unobstructed path home. Beyond the lights was the incline up Woolton Road and he seemed intent on giving himself a good run at it. But, as we raced towards the lights, they began to change.

'You'll not hold him now,' Dad warned Uncle George.

The seriousness in his voice alerted me to the situation and I looked ahead. The lights hovered on amber but Rupert literally had the bit between his teeth and was blinkered in pursuit of his goal. He was in full flow, bearing down on the lights as they changed to red.

There is always a pause between one set of lights turning red and the other set turning green; this gives tail-enders time to clear the junction. But I could see that there were no tail-enders on this occasion, just an empty space in the centre of the junction. The buses, lorries, cars and motorcycles stood in their pole positions on either side of this no-man's-land, waiting for the lights to change. Their impatience to be on their busy way was betrayed by a slight roll forward as they anticipated the green light. But before they could hit their accelerators, we shot out from the side of the junction, the horse-drawn vehicle claiming the no-man's-land for itself. Feet may have jumped for brake pedals, but surely any curses would have evaporated on the lips at the magnificent sight of a working horse in full flight. What a picture he would have made: his proud head held high; his legs pumping and his muscles rippling beneath a shining coat; his straight mane bouncing on his broad neck and powerful shoulders. Only the flecks of foam splashing from his mouth would have given any hint of effort.

I caught sight of the mesmerised motorists. A bus driver broke his trance and with a big grin on his face, looked at me and burst into applause, shaking his head in disbelief. Even the pedestrians in the vicinity turned to admire the spectacle. I heard someone cheer us on with a 'Yee-haa'. Dad stood at the open doorway of the van, doffed his cowboy-like trilby and gave a low sweeping bow, reminiscent of Buffalo Bill at the end of a Wild West Show. 'Thank you! We're here 'til Thursday – try the milk!' he announced as we charged through the junction, leaving a grandstand of awestruck faces in the vacuum to our rear.

It all seemed to happen in slow motion. For a very special extended moment, horsepower gave way to the power of the horse; it was as if, for one last time, the Age of the Motor respectfully acknowledged the Age of the Horse.

We cleared the junction. With a whooping laugh, Dad replaced his hat and turned to me, his face a picture of exuberance with just a hint of relief. 'Wow!' I reciprocated.

'That was lucky,' stated Uncle George, whose concentration on his driving had remained unbroken throughout. I looked back. The spell was broken and the two lines of traffic closed behind us like the Red Sea behind Moses in the Children's Illustrated Bible.

The momentum of the run took Rupert up to the break in the slope while still at a trot. Uncle George pulled him back to a walk as we turned into the narrower side streets that led back to the dairy. The sound of his hooves on the metalled road surface announced our return. We pulled into the stable yard and came to a halt. I followed Dad as he dismounted from the van to chock a wheel. Still chuckling to himself, yet loud enough for the horse to know where he was, Dad walked to the front and slapped Rupert hard but affectionately on his muscular neck while taking hold of the bridle.

'Well, me old fella-me-lad,' he chirped. 'You really enjoyed yerself there, didn't ya?' I moved to the front of the horse and rubbed him on his forehead. I could feel the moist heat emanating from him. It made the orange juice on my fingers turn sticky again. 'I expect thee'll be wantin' a drink after that, won't ya?' Dad continued. The horse raised his head and gave two nods of affirmation and a snort of thanks. Rupert was home again.

1   Dad in the army.

2   Mum and Dad's
    wedding, Garston
    parish church.

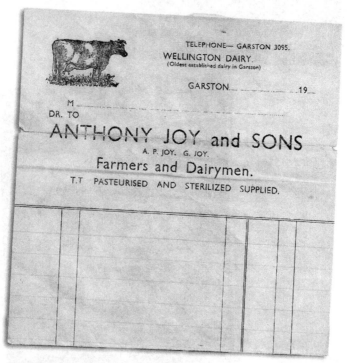

OLDEST ESTABLISHED DAIRY IN GARSTON.

A. JOY & SONS,

Farmers and Cowkeepers,

❖

"WELLINGTON" DAIRY,

GARSTON.

Families supplied at their own Residences with Genuine Milk and Cream.
INSPECTION INVITED.

3   A Wellington Dairy business card.

TELEPHONE— GARSTON 3095.
WELLINGTON DAIRY.
(Oldest established dairy in Garston)

GARSTON................19....

M ....
DR. TO

ANTHONY JOY and SONS

A. P. JOY.   G. JOY.

Farmers and Dairymen.

T.T PASTEURISED AND STERILIZED SUPPLIED.

4   Wellington Dairy headed notepaper.

5 The last hay crop – Joys Field, off Horrocks Avenue, Garston. Uncle George (above) and Dad (below).

6 Dad driving Rupert in the milk float along Garston Old Road, Garston.

7   Dad and a young Danny in Duke Street, Garston.

8   Me on Danny's back (yes!) with my father, my sister
     Ann, and my brother Billy, in Duke Street.

9   Granddad with Danny and Uncle George with
     Rupert and Peggy in Duke Street.

10 Exercising Danny in Duke Street.

11 Granddad and Danny with my father, Ann and Billy.

12 On holiday in Blackpool.

13 Nana and Granddad at the front door of
   No. 37 Wellington Street, Garston.

14 Nana,
   Granddad
   and Arthur
   at home
   in No. 37
   Wellington
   Street.

15 Dad and his dogs in the stable yard.

16 Dad and Granddad outside the Duke of Wellington Hotel, Duke Street.

Chapter Eleven

GOD'S OWN COUNTRY

It was normally at this time of year that we went on holiday to Blackpool – but not this year. It had been just after Easter when Mum and Dad had announced that our annual holiday to Blackpool would have to be cancelled. It was a major disappointment. We simply loved holidaying in Blackpool. It was a magical experience and one to which we looked forward all year. In fact it was second only to Christmas as the highlight of our year. We had protested long and hard at the idea of it being cancelled. But, as she regularly did, Mum had reminded us that Dad's wages were only just enough for us not to qualify for free school meals. 'We're only a tanner above the poverty line,' she had said.

Every summer Dad took one week's holiday while Granddad and Uncle George ran the business. For every year of my life we had taken that holiday in Blackpool. We travelled on the train from Garston to Blackpool North and then took a taxi to the hotel. We always stayed at the same place, the North Bank Hotel, and we always stayed full board so that Mum had a holiday from cooking. On the outside it was painted white and on the inside it was all polished wood and brass. The place shone and there was always an aroma of coffee. It was located on the seafront. You just had to cross the road and the tramlines and you were on the promenade, overlooking the enormous expanse of golden beach.

As well as the beach, promenade and trams there was also the Tower Circus with its water show finale; the Pleasure Beach with its Fun House (and that laughing clown that used to give us all nightmares – but I was too old now for that sort of stuff); the three piers with their shows and slot machines; the Golden Mile of shops, stalls and more slot machines; the Winter Gardens where we had once seen Cliff Richard & The Shadows and the football ground where we went to see a Wild West rodeo show. There was ice cream, candy floss, toffee apples, hot dogs and beefburgers with fried onions, too. Each time we went, we were a year older and so each year we had the strength and the stamina to do more.

Dad and I were having a late lunch at the dairy and I decided to broach the subject of holidays in the hope of eliciting from him some sort of confirmation that we would be returning to Blackpool next year. As we tucked into Nana's bubble 'n' squeak – the chopped and fried remains of the Sunday roast – I asked him how old he was when he first went there for his holidays.

'To Blackpool? Let's see. I would have been just five years old the first time we went there,' he said, 'it was 1925.' He fell silent, chewing on the fried leftovers.

My question seemed to have engaged his mind, but not his vocal chords. I decided to prompt him further. 'Was it much different from today?'

'Well, let's see,' he began again, warming to the subject. 'In those days the trams I saw running along the seafront could only be accessed from the end, not from the side – though there are one or two of those still running today. That year the giant ferris wheel was in Blackpool. It's no longer there, mind you, as it was taken down in the early thirties. Also, I remember there were booths where people would come in and play a piano and ask the audience to sing a song and then try to sell the sheet music to that song. They were songs by Irving Berlin; songs like "What'll I Do" and "Always" and "I Remember".'

He stared into space, smiling to himself. It sounded as if he enjoyed Blackpool as much as I did. But, I still hadn't got him going, so I persevered with my line of questioning. I asked him if he had gone to Blackpool every year, like I had done so far.

'Not every year, no. Me papa was born in the Yorkshire Dales and he used to like going back there whenever he could. In fact we went there the following year, in 1926. That was the year of the railway strike, so a journey that normally took four hours, took ten hours – from Liverpool to Grassington. We had to change at Preston, then Blackburn and then Colne, where we waited for two hours. From there we went on to Skipton and then caught the local train to Grassington. We set off at nine o'clock in the morning and arrived at Grassington at seven o'clock in the evening. We stayed with a lady called Miss Chester. I stayed there for ten days and thoroughly enjoyed it. My father used to take a maximum of twelve days' holiday at a time, so that he was only away for one weekend in the fortnight. We always started our holiday on a Monday and came back a week the following Friday, so that he was back in time to collect the milk money at the weekend. In those days money was scarce.'

Now he was in full flow. He gulped a mouthful of bubble 'n' squeak and carried on talking. 'In 1927 me papa bought his first car, a "Bullnose" Morris Cowley, so he drove us on holiday instead of going by train. That year we went to Grange-over-Sands. The Morris Cowley was a tourer that could hold five – two in the front and three in the back with a bench seat. We kept that Bullnose until 1931 and then we bought a saloon. It was a posher car, but it was not as good as the Bullnose Morris.'

Another pause while another mouthful of leftovers was shovelled into his mouth – and then on again. 'In 1928 we went to Threshfield for a holiday and while we were there your granddad took ill. He was so ill that Nana feared he had pneumonia. I was asleep and didn't find out until the morning, but he had started in the middle of the night and the doctor had been sent for. The doctor kept him in bed for three days while Nana dosed him with whiskey to bring his temperature down. It wasn't much of a holiday for him and he spent most of the rest of the week just walking around Threshfield, getting back on his feet again.'

Pause – bubble 'n' squeak – continue.

'In 1929 we had a different holiday. My Aunty Annie and Uncle Joe had bought a small cottage in North Wales, at a place called Penmachno, four miles from Betws-y-Coed. We had a twelve-day holiday there, with them – Nana and Granddad and me, staying with Aunty Annie, Uncle Joe and my cousin Ivy. Uncle Joe used to go there at weekends. Every other week he would work nights and then go to the cottage on Saturday morning. He worked at Garston Docks, which were owned by the railway company and so he was able to travel by train for one quarter of the fare and he was given three free passes per year. He also used to let it out as a holiday cottage. It was halfway up a mountain and was rather primitive, with an earth closet and no running water, just a stream. Ha! We used to have to boil the water to make sure it was safe to drink. Hell! How times have changed.'

'Now that we have a car, are you going to drive us to Blackpool next year?'

'Well, that's what your mother has in mind, but I'll have to pass my test first. Though once I can drive, we don't necessarily have to go to Blackpool for our holiday. There are other places we can go.'

'Like where?' I had never considered going anywhere else other than Blackpool.

'Well, like the Dales, for example. I've never taken you there before. I think you'd enjoy it. Its God's own country. Not far from Grassington is a little village called Hebden. That's where the Joy family originated from. It's where my great grandfather, Daniel Joy's family lived. I'd like to have a good look around there one day and see if I can trace any of our relatives. You could help me do that, couldn't you?'

'Err, yeah. I suppose so.' From Dad's description I found the idea of seeing 'God's own country' and finding out more about our family to be quite attractive. But would I rather do that than go back to Blackpool? I wanted to know more about my ancestors. 'Who were Daniel's family?'

'I know for sure that two of his brothers, George and Orlando, also came to Liverpool, sometime in the early 1860s. George stayed here and ran a milk business from Barlton Dairy, off Smithdown Road. Orlando married here but returned to Yorkshire with his family.'

'But why come to Liverpool when they were living in "God's own country"?'

'Ha! Well, at that time there were great changes taking place. Most of the farmers in the Dales supplemented their income by working in the lead mines, but that kind of work began to disappear as the mines became exhausted. At the same time, there was the Industrial Revolution and people were moving to the big cities where there was work. In Liverpool there was a growth of industry around the port, including the docks at Garston. Now, all these people working in these new industries needed houses, so new houses were built. And all these new houses needed a daily supply of fresh milk. So, that's why some farmers moved here; there was much more business to be had here than in the Dales. They kept cows in shippons like the one we have. That's why they became known as 'cow keepers' rather than farmers.' Dad broke a cob of bread and began to wipe his plate clean.

'So, if the Joy family moved to Liverpool, why are there still Joys in Yorkshire?'

'Ah, that's because Daniel had other brothers who didn't move to Liverpool and also because Daniel's father, Thomas Joy, had brothers too – who had sons of their own and so it goes on.'

'It sounds very complicated.'

'I know. The further back you go, the more complicated it gets. That's why I'd like to go to the Dales for a holiday, to see if I can work it out. Your granddad still has cousins living there and they tell me that there are many Joy family graves at Burnsall church, so that might be a good place to start. Hey, hang on a second.' Dad went over to Granddad's bureau and began rooting around inside. 'Here it is,' he announced, and produced an old black and white photograph. 'Hole Bottom Farm, Hebden,' he read from the back of the photo. 'Now, look here.' He held out the print for me to see.

It wasn't just a black and white photograph, it was one of those olde worlde ones that have a brown tinge, like something out of a history book. It depicted a group of seven people stood posing outside some sort of farmhouse. The men were all wearing three–piecers and bowler hats, and the women were in pinched bodices with long dresses down to the ankles. It looked like a scene from one of those Charlie Chaplin mad movies.

'That's Anthony, David, Dick and Horatio,' said Dad, reading from the back of the print and then pointing to the male figures.

'What! So there was another Anthony Joy and also a David Joy?'

'Yes. The same names do tend to crop up again and again in family history. Babies are named after their relations – that's why you were christened Anthony. I think that these three – Anthony, David and Dick – were brothers and they would have been Daniel Joy's uncles.'

'Horatio is an unusual name. Who was he?'

Dad sucked on his lip. 'I don't know. He might have been a nephew.'

'Who's the old lady in the wheelchair?'

'I'm not too sure of that either,' Dad laughed. 'She might have been David's wife. I've been told that they were both very old when they got married.'

'And this "Hole Bottom Farm" - is that where the Joys lived?'

'That's where some of them lived, yes. It would be interesting to go and find it and see who lives there now, don't you think?'

'Yeah. It would be like trying to solve a jigsaw puzzle, except with people rather than jigsaw pieces.'

'Right then,' declared Dad. 'We'll see what we can do about it.'

Wow! A quest! Exploring the Dales in search of our ancestors. It captured my imagination. I could visualise the two of us trekking around the countryside, tracing steps, knocking on doors, in and out of churches, examining gravestones. It all sounded like great fun. I decided I could probably give Blackpool a miss – well, maybe, just for one more year – and spend a holiday in God's own country instead.

Chapter Twelve

RAISING THE FLAG

As the Duke Street Kids, we had devised a way of testing our maturing physical capabilities with our own version of weightlifting. In the lean-to there would often be full or part-full crates of milk, waiting to be loaded for delivery or to be stored in the walk-in refrigerator. Each crate would take twenty one-pint bottles. We would increase the weight by adding bottles and then compete with each other as to who could dead lift the greatest weight. Bonzo could lift a full crate easily. But, over a period of time, Tubs and I had increased the weight until we were just a few bottles short of a full crate. We had planned to see if we could lift a full crate of milk before I finished my sleepover week at the dairy. Today was my last day.

I finished my lunch and walked down Duke Street to Tubs' house. He lived over the shops in James Street with his large family, consisting of his parents, his two younger sisters and two older brothers and his grandmother. They were referred to by everyone and his dog as 'The Tubs Family', but Tubs was not their real family name – that was 'Schwimmer'. They were called 'Tubs' because the whole family was of the same portly character. And what is more, they all answered to the name Tubs; the kids and the father as if it were their Christian name and the two women as if it were their surname (both Mrs Tubs). Indeed, in public they would call each other Tubs! In idle moments I would speculate on what they might call each other in the privacy of their home. Surely if everyone was called Tubs it would get very confusing.

I found Tubs sitting on his step playing with his grandmother's magnifying glass, experimenting and seeing how different things burned.

'Alright Tubs la! Are you coming to see if we can lift a full crate?'

'Alright la! Erm, yeah. But I'm going to have me dinner now. I'll come up after that. I won't be long.'

'Okay den.'

'Here. Have a look at me new badges,' he insisted, handing me the biscuit tin that housed his collection. I prised the lid off and there was an awful smell of bad eggs. 'Phwar! Berloody 'ell!' I swore with disgust.

Tubs burst into his usual big goofy laughter. 'I just apple tarted in it!'

'Yer dirty git.'

He laughed even more. 'Hey, watch this!' He picked a big black and green bogey from his nose, wiped it on the ground and proceeded to focus the sun's rays on it through the magnifying glass. After a moment it snapped, crackled and popped like a hot Rice Krispie cooking in its own juices. As it began to smoke, I recognised the smell.

'That's burning hoof! Like in the smithy!' I cried.

'S'not,' laughed Tubs.

Just then his mum called him in for his dinner. He said he was only having a sandwich. 'See yer in a mo,' he promised as he went inside.

I walked slowly back up the street and turned into the stable yard. Dad's new car had arrived. It wasn't new. He had bought it second-hand from his cousin, Doug. It was a Hillman Imp and as cars go, it was small. Until Dad passed his test he could only drive the car when accompanied by Granddad, so it was being garaged in the stable yard. It sat there in a corner of the yard like a grinning little, well, imp; something from an alien world.

I walked around it, studying it. The blue metal and shiny chrome contrasted so sharply with its surrounds of cobbled yard, dirty brick walls, rusting lean-to, and painted-wood float. I touched it. It felt hard, cold, and dead, unlike the soft living warmth of a horse. I smelled it. Outside, it smelled of petrol but when I opened a door, the inside smelled of plastic. Its smell made me feel nauseous. I turned away from it in search of the comfortable smell of hay and horse muck.

As I turned, Tubs stepped towards me with an imaginary knife held high in his hand, making high-pitched screaming sounds with each pretend stab at me.

'Shee-it!' I swore, as he took me by surprise. He gave one of his goofy laughs and then croaked 'welcome to the Bates Motel,' in imitation of an old woman.

I asked what he was on about. He told me about a film he had sneaked a look at on the television the night before. 'It was called *Psycho*,' he said. 'It was about this mad bloke called Norman Bates who dresses up like an old woman and murders people!'

He went on to describe and enact scenes from the film in great detail, playing the part of Norman Bates. His high-pitched screams were meant to be the 'stabbing' soundtrack. He made it sound disturbingly scary; the sort of images that would make you cower under the bedclothes at night. He had managed to see it because the bedroom he shared with his brothers was right next to the living room. His mum and dad were out at the pub and his gran had fallen asleep in front of the set.

Tubs commented on the new car. He said that his uncle had a car and that he thought it was cool to own one. His envy somewhat softened my attitude to the Imp, although he did go on to claim that his uncle's car was an E-Type Jaguar, but I didn't believe that. We turned our attention to the milk crates, standing in the lean-to.

Although Tubs was often the butt of many jokes (some of which were of his own making), he did command our respect in activities where his weight was an advantage. Previously, we both had managed to lift an eighteen-bottled crate and now we were about to attempt a full twenty-bottle lift. I remembered watching the Olympic weightlifters on the television the year before and Dad pointing out how they kept their backs straight and lifted with their legs. This time I adopted a similar stance in front of the full crate. Tubs burst into laughter.

'What's so funny?' I demanded.

'You – sticking yer arse out like a monkey!'

'This is how the weightlifters on the telly do it,' I explained.

'Oh yeah, sure,' he scoffed, still laughing.

I readopted my squat position and braced myself. As I began to lift, Tubs' laughter stopped. I slowly straightened my legs and stood up, bearing the full weight of the crate. Then, after a slight pause to make the point, I carefully lowered it back to the ground.

'Yeeeeeeeeeees!' I yelled triumphantly. 'I did it! It's a doddle!'

'Let me try,' said Tubs, eager not to be outdone. He quickly positioned himself, bending over the crate. He put on his serious face and began to heave. But he was still trying to lift with his back.

'You won't do it like that,' I said. 'You have to stick yer arse out like I did.'

He adjusted his position and tried to squat, but his waistline and his thick thighs made it difficult for him. He tried to lift again, his face turning red with the effort. His pants were tight across his backside and the seams were under great tension. The milk bottles rattled as the crate began to lift off the ground. All of a sudden he gave up an absolute thunderclap of a fart that would have put the horses to shame. He released the crate with a crash and the two of us fell about in rude laughter. It took us what seemed like an age to get our breath back.

When we had finally recovered, Tubs declared that his sides were too sore to try lifting the crate again. But, with my newfound confidence, I suggested we go and find something else to lift.

We walked from the stable yard towards the dairy. As we came to the jigger that separated the two premises, I could see Dad in the covered yard. He was also busy moving crates of milk. I wanted to tell him of my achievement but I wasn't totally sure it would have met with his approval. Instead, my attention was caught by what turned out to be a paving flag that had been left propped up at the end of the usually clutter-free jigger.

Tubs had spotted it too. 'What's that?'

'Dunno,' I shrugged. 'Let's have a dekko.'

We walked to the end of the jigger and curiously inspected the flag. It hadn't been there the day before but it was now leaning against someone's back wall. It was not like the smooth quarried stone on which it was standing. This was a modern concrete paving flag with a harsh gravel upper surface that gave it edges like mini sharks' teeth.

'Do you think I could lift that?' I half-whispered to Tubs.

'Naaaaa,' he replied. And then dared, 'Go on then.'

The flag stood about as high as my waist. I decided to try to pull it into an upright position to get a feel for its weight. When I placed my hands behind it, the gravel finish immediately bit into my soft boyish skin. I braced my toes against the bottom edge and tugged backwards. Nothing happened. It was a dead weight. Tubs laughed at my impotence.

I set myself again and this time used the strength of my upper arms to better effect. The top edge of the flag began to move away from the wall. I could feel the gravel biting deeper into the sensitive skin of my fingers. It reached an upright position and I gave a confident laugh. But that brief confidence evaporated as the momentum of the flag took it past the perpendicular and I realised to my horror that it was falling towards me.

I did not have the strength to halt its arc and I could not get out of the way quick enough. It all happened so suddenly.

Before I knew it, the flag had knocked me to the ground and was lying on top of me, pinning me from my hips downwards.

'Tubs! Help me.'

Tubs ran up and grabbed an edge. He braced himself and heaved. Nothing. He changed his position and stood astride me. I had the indignity of looking up at his broad backside as he braced himself to lift. As he began to strain, the thought of one of his thunder farts flashed through my mind but I swore that if he got me out of this mess I'd never joke about his size ever again.

'I can't lift it, Deejay,' he said between clenched teeth.

'Quick, get me dad.'

Helpless, I watched him waddle off back down the jigger towards the dairy door as fast as his tubby legs would carry him. Please, please, please let Dad be still there, I prayed to myself.

He stopped at the doorway and shouted 'Mr Joy!'

'Ello!' I heard Dad reply. It was such a relief to hear his voice. I could feel the concrete flag grinding into the flesh of my hands, my hips, my knees and my ankles, but I knew I only had to hang on for a few seconds more before rescue.

'Your Dave wants yer!'

Wha! I could not believe my ears. My heart sank at the enormity of his understatement. Here I lay beneath half a ton of concrete and he says: 'Your Dave wants yer.' The gravel is flaying my skin and grinding my bones and all he can say is: 'Your Dave wants yer.' I am pinned, helpless, being slowly crushed to death and the best he can muster is: 'Your Dave wants yer.' Clearly, there was only tenpence to Tubs' shilling.

'Well, tell him to come here then.'

'He can't.'

'Why not?'

'Cos he's gorra concrete flag on top of him.'

(Ah – at last!)

'What!' Seconds later, Dad appeared at the doorway to the dairy and looked down the jigger to where I lay. 'Berloody 'ell!'

'Dad!' I cried. And with that the dam burst – my lips blubbed, my chin puckered and the tears flowed down my face. (Blubbing in front of your mates was an unthinkable weakness, but for some reason it was okay if your parents were present.) Dad ran towards me. He was only of slight build but he lifted that concrete flag like it was made of cardboard. The concrete sharks' teeth blunted themselves against his leathery, calloused working man's hands. 'Berloody 'ell!' He swore again as he saw the blood oozing from the cuts and grazes on my hands, arms and legs.

He scooped me up in one movement. The smell of him was immediately comforting. It might have been the smell of sweat, of horses and of Brylcreem, but it was also the smell of safety; safe in my dad's arms. He carried me at a half run into the dairy and I could hear Tubs running along behind us saying, 'I tried to lift it off him Mr Joy, but it was too heavy.'

By the time we had run through the covered yard and vaulted up the stone steps into the kitchen, my crying was in full flow as the numbing effect of the initial shock wore off. It was a red pain, as if I had cuts on the angle of every bony joint. As Dad sat me down on the dresser next to the sink, Nana and Granddad came shuffling out of the house to investigate the commotion.

'What's happened?' Granddad asked.

'He was in the entry with a berloody concrete flag on top of him,' replied Dad.

'There'll be no swearing in this house,' lectured Nana.

'And how did that happen?' Granddad continued.

'He was tryin' to lift it,' said Tubs, standing in the kitchen doorway.

'Has he broken anything?' Granddad asked Dad.

'I think he cracked the flag,' interjected Tubs, wearing his serious face.

'I don't think so,' said Dad, ignoring Tubs. 'Looks like he just has some bad grazes.' He looked at me and asked, 'Where does it hurt?'

My crying was coming under control and I managed to sob, 'Me hand.'

Dad began to examine my hand. As he gently prised open my fist, a two-inch strip of raw bleeding skin dropped and dangled from the base of my finger like a piece of red apple peel. Unnoticed by me, as I had tried to fend off the falling flag, the gritty concrete edge had stripped the skin from my middle finger, from the tip down to the palm. The pain of this particular injury had been masked in the general hurt I was experiencing all over my body. But now I wailed at the sight of it.

'Berloody 'ell!' said Dad.

'Don't swear in the house, Eric,' insisted Nana.

Dad swivelled me over the sink and held my hand under the cold tap as he turned it full on. The swirling jet of icy water immediately turned pink as it mixed with my blood. The result of this was that my crying reached a new, previously uncharted, octave.

The next thing I remembered was Nana appearing with a pair of scissors. 'Hold his hand still, Eck, while I cut off the skin.' That immediately grabbed my attention. My crying stopped in its tracks.

'Berloody 'ell!' I exclaimed.

'Don't you swear in my house, young man,' scolded Nana.

But it wasn't my nana I was seeing – it was Norman Bates. Moving slowly towards his victim, dressed as an old woman with a bun of hair and a pair of scissors – just like Tubs had described. Only this time he was going to cut off my skin! I loved my nana dearly, but now I could only see this *Psycho* old woman shuffling forward with this pair of lethal scissors, closing in on my flesh. I could almost hear the stabbing soundtrack. Dad held my hand still as I struggled to be free. The scissors closed in on either side of my dangling human apple-peel skin.

'Noooooo!' I screamed as with one snip I was separated from my skin.

I was expecting agony, but to my surprise and great relief I felt nothing – of course, the skin was dead. It had looked a lot worse than it actually was. And I wasn't the only one who thought so. As the scissors snipped and my flesh dropped into the sink, there was a groan from the doorway and Tubs hit the tiled kitchen floor in a dead faint. A fraction of a second later, his inert body let rip with a thunderous fart.

'Berloody 'ell!' said Nana.

Chapter Thirteen

SHELL SHOCKED

Dad put me on 'light duties' for a week or so while my finger healed, the gauze bandage constantly smelling of Germolene. Nevertheless, whenever I was at the dairy, I stuck to him like goose grass.

Occasionally, Dad would help out with the maintenance of the church graveyard. Up until recently the whole site had been completely overgrown, but a group of volunteers were now claiming it back from nature. The church had decided to splash out on one of the new petrol-driven hover mowers, but first the overgrown vegetation had to be flailed and removed. Dad had volunteered to do the raking off as we had two big wooden hay rakes that were ideal for the job. I thought this might be a good opportunity to get a closer look at the sparrowhawk we had spotted whilst doing the bottom round. So, on a balmy August afternoon, I accompanied him on the relatively short walk from the dairy to the church. He carried both rakes, one on each shoulder.

As we walked under the bridge, the church steps came into view. I daren't tell Dad about cycling down the steps, but I couldn't resist mentioning them. I asked him if he knew the story about the drunk falling down the steps. He said he hadn't heard that one but he had a better one. 'It was when the last vicar was here,' he explained. 'Because the path down to the lychgate was so long, they started using a wheeled trolley to carry the coffins. Well, one day the trolley broke loose and went careering down the path with the mourners in full pursuit, led by the vicar. When it reached the bottom of the path the trolley went through the lychgate and carried on down Banks Road. The vicar ran into the nearest shop to get help. The only one open on a Sunday was the chemist. The vicar raced inside and said to the pharmacist – "can you give me something to stop this coffin!"'

It was only when he began laughing that I realised this wasn't a true story at all. I rolled my eyes at his pathetic pun. 'Da-ad!' I groaned. He laughed so much that he started coffin – I mean coughin'.

From the entrance gate on Church Road the church towered above us, perched on a sandstone outcrop. Being a choirboy, I knew that this church was built in 1877 and that it was the third church to be built on this site. We climbed the five flights of steps. I couldn't believe that I had actually ridden down them. I counted them – there were twenty-one in total. When we reached the top, we were level with the railway that was carried by the bridge over Church Road. The church was bounded on one side by the railway and to the rear by the 'gaswerks'. A huge gasometer filled the sky behind the church. According to Encyclopedia Eck-tannica, it was erected in 1893 and it held four million cubic feet of gas. I tried to imagine the gasometer filled with four million feet; no wonder gas was smelly.

'That's what made the church such an important target during the war,' Dad explained. 'If the Germans could locate the church, then they could bomb the railway line to the docks or they could bomb the docks themselves or they could bomb the gasworks. If they could have dropped a shell on the gasometer, then they wouldn't have had to worry about the docks because if the gasworks had gone up then they would have taken most of Garston with them.'

'Tell me the story about Mr Newgass,' I prompted him.

'Harold Newgass? He was a lieutenant in the Royal Navy Volunteer Reserve, and he was the man who saved Garston when the Germans finally did manage to drop a landmine on the gasworks in November 1940. The landmine smashed through the top of gasholder No. 1, allowing the gas to escape, but the parachute snagged before it hit the bottom, so it didn't explode. Most people in this part of Garston were evacuated for a couple of days while the bomb was being defused. Harold Newgass was the bomb disposal officer who had to climb into the gasholder to disarm the bomb. The local fire brigade lent him their breathing masks but they only had six and each one only had enough air to last thirty minutes. So, he climbed in there six times, each time doing a bit more work until at last the bomb was rendered harmless. He was a hero and he was awarded the George Cross.'

I tried to imagine what it must have been like to climb into a gasholder while there was an unexploded bomb in it. Mr Newgass must have been very brave – I'd have just run a mile. 'When the gasholder had been repaired, I think I know what they refilled it with,' I mused.

'Oh, really? What?'

'They refilled it with new-gas!'

'Ah, very funny and I don't think,' chuckled Dad.

We walked down the churchyard to the Joy family grave. It lay just beyond the shade of a young lime tree. Dad brushed some of the moss off the stone with his hand. He read aloud from the carved headstone. 'In affectionate remembrance of Daniel Joy, who departed this life February 3rd 1896, aged 70 years.'

'What relation was he to me, then?'

'He was your great-great-granddad.'

I read out the rest of the epitaph to Daniel. It was in the form of a short poem:

A Father most dearly beloved,

Now free from all sorrow and pain.

By death from our circle removed,

Our hope is to meet him again.

'Not exactly the most uplifting of sentiments,' observed Dad. I asked him what he meant. 'Well, it basically says he was better off dead and so will we all be! It's not what you would describe as being full of the Joys of life, is it,' he laughed. 'I hope they come up with something more fitting for me.'

'Like what?'

'Oh, I don't know.' He paused, then laughed, 'Something like: "Eric Joy – Hoof-Hearted!"'

'What? Do you really mean that? Is that what you want on your gravestone?'

'No. I can't have that. I don't think the church would allow it,' he smiled. And then reflected, 'I've never really thought about it before. Perhaps it's time I did.' He looked at the gravestone in silence.

After a moment of contemplation I piped up. 'I know. How about: "I'm NOT old"?' We both laughed at that.

'Actually, that's probably all there is room for now,' said Dad, referring to the fully engraved stone. He read out the names and told me what he knew about each member of the family. Ellen Gertrude Joy, died 1891, aged five months; Anthony Joy, died 1937; Ann Jane Joy, died 1951; George Price, died 1966; and Flora, died 1969. I had not known any of the people whose names appeared there except for my Great Auntie Flora. She had died in January. She was the first person I had known who had died (President Kennedy didn't count). I had felt very sad that I would not see her again, but I had been very grown up about it and had not cried. If I closed my eyes I could still see her face and hear her voice – 'Ee, arr Der-vid'. She was a large jolly lady with a Yorkshire accent.

The grave now overlooked the entrance gates to the Stalbridge Dock. 'It wasn't always like that,' mused Dad, looking down Dale Street. 'The plot was chosen because it overlooked the fields of Dale Farm, where the Joy family had farmed since 1863. In those days the family had a dairy in Railway Street, just across the road from the church. They had to move from Dale Farm when Stalbridge Dock was built in 1910. They moved up to the land that iused to be called

The Avenue, but we had to give that up when the Corpy needed land to build new houses after the war.'

He said that there was still room in the plot, just as long as everyone else was cremated and that this is where he would end up as well. I asked him about Mum.

'Oh, she won't want to go in with the Joys,' he snorted. 'She wants to go in the Atherton grave, in Woolton.' I asked why that was. 'Well, you see, when we were first married, we lived at the dairy with your nana and granddad. But, well, living together in a small house is not always easy and your mum and my mum, erm, did not, er, get on very well. Eventually, after we'd had Ann, we bought two-one-eight and moved there. Alice says she doesn't want to be put in a hole to spend the rest of eternity with Nana and Granddad,' Dad laughed, 'she says one lifetime is long enough, thank you very much.'

I thought about that for a while. I thought about the interaction between my mum and my grandparents. For as long as I could remember there had been something about it that made you feel a bit uncomfortable but I was never able to put my finger on it. I had just ignored it - it was adult stuff. But, now it started to make sense; a piece of the jigsaw. It also made me think that maybe Ann wasn't just Granddad's favourite simply because she was the oldest; perhaps it was because when she was born, she lived at the dairy.

From behind us came a guttural hawking and we turned to see Mr Isaiah Houghton winding his way between the gravestones towards us. 'Isaiah' was not his real name; it was his nickname. Having lost his right eye when he was caught in a shell blast during the last war, he now wore a glass eye which floated around in the socket and made it look as if 'one Isaiah than the other'. He had volunteered to maintain the graveyard using the new hover mower and had already cut down the vegetation with a flail mower the church had hired in. He and Dad were going to spend the afternoon raking off. As I knew he spent a lot of time in the graveyard, I asked him about the sparrowhawk and whether it was indeed nesting in the bell tower, as *The Observer's Book of Birds* said they usually nested in trees – but only sometimes on ledges. He told me that they had raised a brood of two and that he had seen the family perching on the gasometer gantry. He said that the bell tower was being repaired and cleaned out and that yesterday he had seen the old nest amongst the debris left by the workmen.

'Go into the church and ask Miss Radcliffe,' he suggested, seeing my obvious interest. 'If it's still around, she'll know where it is.' Miss Radcliffe was a Garston legend. She had spent her whole life serving the church and its community. She had taught my mum at Sunday school. Although people called her 'Miss Radcliffe' or 'Agnes' to her face, most Garstonians affectionately referred to her as 'Aggie-Rack'. One of Mum's prized possessions was a book called *Cargoes to Garston*. It was a book of poems by Aggie-Rack.

I knew her because she helped out in the vestry on Sundays, getting the choirboys robed and ready for the service. On one occasion she had shown us a piece of old cord that she had in her hymn book and she told us the story behind it. This was a piece of the parachute cord that had snagged on the gasholder and prevented the landmine from exploding and sending most of Garston to kingdom come (forever and ever, amen.) Miss Radcliffe had been a

fire warden on duty at the church and the gasworks when
the bomb had been dropped. She had refused to leave her
post and abandon the church. So, when the bomb had been
disarmed, Mr Newgass had given her a piece of the parachute cord. She still had that same piece of cord kept safely
in her hymn book. It marked the page of a hymn called
'Jesus, United by Grace'. After she had showed us the cord,
I made a point of looking at the hymn. There was a verse
that talked about a cord:

> Still let us own our common Lord
> And bear thine easy yoke,
> A band of love, a threefold cord,
> Which never can be broke.

The words were by Charles Wesley and the music was called
'St Agnes' – very fitting, I thought. When I had related Aggie-
Rack's story to Mum and Dad, they had smiled knowingly
and replied in unison, 'Ah, The Lord works in mysterious
ways.'

I left Dad and Isaiah to get on with the raking and I went
back to the church in search of Aggie-Rack. As I stood
outside the church doors, I craned back my neck and looked
straight up at the bell tower, which, well, towered above me.
If the clouds were moving in the right direction there was
a trick of the eye you could experience. The clouds made it
look like the tower was falling over, on top of you. I laughed
to myself at the queasiness the illusion stirred and then ran
into the church to escape being crushed to death.

Inside I found Aggie-Rack at the back of the church

repairing prayer books. The sun was shining on her through the stained glass of the great south window. For a moment she looked like Joseph in the Children's Illustrated Bible. Then she stepped out of the multicoloured light and I could see that she was dressed in her usual uniform of blue with a white blouse. It wasn't any particular uniform, it was just her personal uniform and she was an instantly recognisable figure because of it.

'Hello Agg ... erm, Miss Radcliffe,' I said, and she greeted me with a warm smile. I repeated what Isaiah (or rather, Mr Houghton) had said and asked if she knew where the old nest was. She told me that all the rubbish from the bell tower was piled at the bottom of the bell tower steps, ready to be taken away.

'What's left of the nest is in a cardboard box with other rubbish,' she said. 'It's all a bit messy now, and there's a broken egg.' An egg! Now that was an unexpected piece of good news. I had never before seen a sparrowhawk egg, broken or otherwise. Miss Radcliffe asked after my mum, we exchanged a few pleasantries and then I went to the bell tower.

Just outside the door leading to the bell tower steps there was a small pile of rubbish, made up of broken and splintered timber, chicken wire covered in pigeon droppings, cardboard boxes, old newspapers and broken slates. I rooted through the boxes until I found what appeared to be an untidy bundle of sticks and twigs. I prised the bundle open and found a thin broken layer of downy feathers. Then, in amongst the down I caught sight of a piece of eggshell. It was cream coloured with reddish-brown blotches. I cupped my fingers underneath and carefully pulled away the shell and the down that was stuck to it. As I picked off the small wispy feathers, I realised to my great delight that the two halves of a broken eggshell were stuck to and covering the two ends of a second, whole egg; an egg within an egg, as it were.

This was a real find, but also a bit of a moral dilemma. I knew birds' eggs were protected by law and those of birds of prey in particular. But this one wasn't in a nest, it was in a load of rubbish that was about to be tipped. Also, I certainly wasn't going to be disturbing any bird to get it. It appeared to me that it would be whoever had cleaned the nest out of the bell tower who had been the one who had broken the law – not me. There was nothing in the Children's Illustrated Bible about taking birds' eggs but I decided to get permission to take it – just to be on the safe side.

I placed the two broken pieces of shell back on to the whole egg and with this messy handful, went off in search of Aggie-Rack once more. She had no formal position in the church but everyone treated her as if she was the church.

'Vicars will come and vicars will go, but Aggie-Rack is the rock on which this church is built!' Mum had once declared. I pointed out that the church was built on sandstone. 'That may be,' she replied, 'but if anyone is sure of going to heaven when their time is up, it's Aggie-Rack.'

So, if I could say that Aggie-Rack said I could take the egg, then that would be good enough. That would be like getting permission from the highest authority. I found her where I had left her, still repairing prayer books at the back of the church. I showed her the messy 'broken' egg shells and as innocently as possible, asked if I could take them home to look at through a magnifying glass. She looked at the egg shells in my hand

and then looked into my eyes. But it felt like more than that. It felt like she was looking into my soul. I swallowed hard and felt myself wilting under that gaze. She knew. I had been very careful not to lie, but she knew anyway. And what's more, she knew that I knew that she knew.

Then she smiled. 'As long as your mum won't mind,' she said. I explained that Mum was used to me bringing home bits of animals and plants. 'Very well then,' she concluded. I thanked her and then left. On my way out I avoided looking in the direction of the altar – just to be on the safe side. I took my find over to Dad and Isaiah. I told them I had Miss Radcliffe's permission to take the 'broken' egg shells. They gave it a quick glance but did not see through the disguise.

I placed the egg behind the family gravestone for safekeeping while I explored the rest of the graveyard. Looking down towards the south docks, I tried to imagine what that view would have been like one hundred years before, but it was difficult to visualise it as farmed fields. I looked at the names on the gravestone. I wondered how many Joys had stood exactly where I was standing now, had looked at the view and had wondered about their predecessors as I was now wondering about mine.

My exploration of the graveyard did not turn up anything particularly interesting. There was the rosebay willowherb, with its bright purple flowers. Dad said that it was also called 'fireweed', because during the war it was the first plant to grow on bombsites. I preferred its other name: 'Joy of the Heavens'. I thought that was a very appropriate flower to be growing by the family grave. The other splash of colour was contributed by clumps of ragwort. At this time of year it was covered in vivid black and yellow striped cinnabar moth caterpillars, feeding on the leaves. I knew that their colour was a warning sign, as their bodies stored the poison contained in the ragwort leaves they were eating. I was careful not to touch them.

However, neither of these finds was as interesting as the sparrowhawk egg. I was eager to get it home. As I explored the graveyard, I planned what I would do with it. I knew that to keep an egg you needed to 'blow' it, otherwise it would just go rotten. Uncle George knew how to blow an egg as he did it to make dummy pigeon eggs. He used dummy eggs to stop his pigeons from breeding too quickly. He blew the yolk out and then painted the empty shell with clear varnish to harden it. He then substituted the dummies for the real eggs in the pigeons' nesting boxes. While the pigeon was sitting on eggs it would not lay any more. But I had never witnessed how he did it. I had only ever seen the finished product.

Isaiah and Dad piled all the cut vegetation at the rear of the church. Dad had said that there were too many weeds in it, like ragwort, for it to be of any use for feeding to the horses. So, Isaiah said he would make a compost heap out of it. With that job done, Dad and I walked back to the dairy, him carrying the two rakes on his shoulders and me carrying the egg in my cupped hands.

I told him how much I had always wanted to see a sparrowhawk egg and thanked him for taking me with him to the church. He said that if there was ever anything that I wanted like that, then I should always ask – the worst he could do was say 'No'. Then he laughed and started singing 'With Love From Me To You'. I joined in with the fish and chip responses:

If there's anything that you want,

Fish and chips.

If there's anything I can doooo,

Wrap 'em up,

Just call on me and I'll send 'em along ...

... with salt and vinegar too-oo-oo, with salt and vinegar too!

When we arrived back at the dairy I went into the cold room where Nana kept her eggs, butter and meat. I found an empty egg box, placed the sparrowhawk egg in it and put it into one of the drawers. I then went next door to see if Uncle George was in. I found him in his pigeon loft. I told him I had an egg that I wanted to blow, if he would show me how it was done.

'What kind of egg?' He asked.

'Erm, it might be a sparrow – ahem – I think,' I replied, coughing the word 'hawk' under my breath.

'Hm. We'll use a hen's egg. Come into the kitchen.'

We went into the house but there was no sign of Aunty Mary. 'Out visitin',' explained Uncle George. He took one hen's egg from a wooden bowl piled high with eggs of every shade, from cream to brown. He then took a large darning needle out of a dresser drawer.

'Use an ordinary sewing needle or pin for the sparrow egg,' he advised. He turned the point of the needle into one end of the egg, using it like a drill. Eventually, he applied a bit of pressure to the needle and it broke through the shell. 'Put your thumb over that hole while you make one in the other end.' This second hole he made slightly larger than the first by chipping away at the edge of the shell surrounding the hole. He then used the needle to prod around inside the egg. 'To break up the yolk,' he explained, 'makes it easier to come out.'

With that, he placed a glass tumbler on the dresser and tipped the egg over it. Some of its contents dripped into the tumbler under the force of gravity. Then Uncle George applied his lips to the smaller hole and gave a sharp blow with his cheeks. The rest of the yellow yolk and clear albumen plopped into the tumbler. 'It's as easy as that,' he concluded. 'Just be a bit more gentle with a sparrow's egg.'

He took a bottle of milk and topped up the tumbler to over halfway. He gave this mixture a stir with a fork and then downed it in three big gulps. 'Does you good,' he announced, seeing the disgust on my face.

I thanked Uncle George and excused myself as tactfully as possible, trying to avoid giving the impression that I was in a hurry to leave. I went straight back to the cold room to put my newly acquired knowledge to use. I retrieved my egg box from the chest of drawers and then rooted around for whatever else I could find to do the job. There were no needles to be found but instead I selected Dad's clickers awl, a tool for putting stitching holes in leather. It had a sharp point and a wooden handle. There was also an old copy of the *Liverpool Echo* and one of Dad's *Horse & Hound* magazines. I chose the *Echo* as I thought that it would be more absorbent than the glossy magazine. Spreading it out on the slate slab, I carefully arranged the tools of my work on top of it: the egg box, the broken eggshell, the awl and, of course, the sparrowhawk egg. I turned it in my fingers. It was like a precious jewel – perfectly made. And it was mine.

I stared at the rich reddish-brown blotches, dots and squiggles that covered its surface. Although it had a smooth surface, its markings made it look like the surface of a full moon with contrasting areas of dark and light, like the shadows of craters and mountains. As I stared, for a moment I thought I saw a face in the pattern – it was the face of Aggie-Rack. In that instant she looked right at me with those penetrating eyes. I blinked away the image and quickly got back to my task.

Working over the newspaper I took the awl in one hand and the egg in the other and began to drill into one end of the egg by gently twisting the awl back and forth, as Uncle George had done. After a few minutes of this, the point of the awl pierced through the shell, creating a perfectly round hole. I placed my thumb over this hole, turned the egg over and repeated the process at the other end. Once I had a second hole, I widened it by gently chipping away at the shell edge with the point of the awl.

This was progressing splendidly. As I worked I reflected on how well my plan had gone. The initial find was just a bit of luck but I took pride in the fact that I had seen what others had missed. The broken-egg disguise was perfect. I hadn't lied to Aggie-Rack so she was okay with it and I'd gotten out of the church without being struck by lightning, so my guess was that God was alright with it. I hadn't lied to Dad or Isaiah and they were alright with it. And by my reckoning, I hadn't lied to Uncle George – ahem! I was feeling pretty pleased with myself and I couldn't wait to share my secret treasure with the Duke Street Kids – they'd be so impressed.

When the second hole was large enough I prodded around inside the shell with the awl to break the yolk. I inverted the egg over the newspaper, placed my lips against the smaller hole and gave a gentle blow. Nothing happened. I did some further prodding with the awl and this time firmly sealed my lips around the small hole and gave a good hard blow.

What disgorged on to the newspaper was not the mixture of yolk and albumen I had expected. This was not the egg of a domestic chicken, intended for human consumption. This was the egg of a wild bird, intended for hatching another wild bird.

What disgorged on to the newspaper was a bloody soup of aborted embryo. Realisation and shock hit me simultaneously. The realisation hit me in the brain – I should have known that this is what would have happened. However, the shock hit me in the stomach: I threw up. I threw up over everything on the newspaper: the bloody soup, the broken egg shell, the awl and the egg box. The sight and smell of this made me retch again. As I did so, my body convulsed and my fingers shattered the egg they were holding and I dropped the broken remains on to the newspaper.

I ran out of the cold room to escape the sight and smell of the horrid mess. I gulped in fresh air. There was no one in the kitchen so I went in there to rinse my mouth under the cold tap. I decided there and then that I'd have to get rid of everything and not tell anyone about this.

I walked back to the cold room and held my nose as I went inside. I could see that the vomit had not spread beyond the newspaper. So, after picking the awl out of the awful soup, with my free hand (I was still holding my nose) I managed to wrap up the newspaper and carry it out to the bin. I only let go of my nose to remove the bin lid. I then retrieved the awl and washed it under the kitchen tap before returning it to the drawer in the cold room.

All my carefully worked plans had come to nought. Maybe Mum and Dad were right when they said, 'The Lord works in mysterious ways'. Maybe he really did.

Chapter Fourteen

THE QUICK AND THE DEAD

My experience with the sparrowhawk egg ended any thoughts I may have harboured about starting an egg collection, but it in no way diminished my enjoyment of birds. My favourite place for birdwatching was the old stable. It had a first floor that was once used as a hayloft. The external doors to the loft hatch had long since disappeared, leaving an open access for swallows to fly in and build their nest on the back wall, just below the wooden roof beam. The same pair seemed to come back every year and always managed to raise two broods. While the parents were busy raising a second brood, the offspring from the first brood would hang around the stable yard, chittering away, like teenagers with nothing to do. I would often climb up the wall-mounted ladder into the hayloft and hide behind a couple of old bales, watching the swallows sweep in and out through the open hatch.

They were beautifully streamlined birds with the longest of forked tails. Their rich blue-black colour was complemented by a red chin and a blue throat. They looked like they had been eating strawberry jam and spilled some of it down their chins and on to their blue bibs. Granddad had told me that if a farmer destroys a swallow's nest, then his cows will yield bloody milk. The Encyclopedia Eck-tannica said that although this was an old farmers' tale, it did have some grounding in truth in that swallows eat flying insects that can spread disease in cattle. Another of Granddad's old farmers' tales was that when winter came, swallows all flew into ponds or lakes and would not emerge again until spring. Of course that was before bird migration was understood. It boggled my mind to think that the very swallows I was watching had flown here from somewhere in southern Africa and in doing so had crossed the Sahara Desert – amazing!

They would catch their prey of flying insects by hawking after them and taking them in mid-air. The younger birds would take some of the flies that were attracted to the midden but the adults were bringing their insects in from the goodsies. They would come in, skimming the rooftops on Wellington Street, head straight for the side of the Duke of Wellington Hotel and then, at the last possible second, wheel around one hundred and eighty degrees to dive over the stable yard and up into the hayloft. Once inside, they would apply the air brakes and pull up to the dried mud lip of the cup-shaped nest, to be met by an explosion of chattering, gaping mouths. They would deposit their load in the biggest mouth and then turn to exit the hayloft in search of more food.

I had found myself a comfortable spot just inside the open hayloft hatch. I sat on the floor beside a bale and covered myself in loose hay. After some initial hesitation, the swallows resumed their feeding routine. This second brood was almost ready to fledge. Looking over my shoulder I had some excellent views of them, like the Dam Busters, swooping low over the stable yard and then in through the hatch. As I looked out of the hatch I saw Dad and Uncle George come into the yard and walk over to Danny's stable. Danny had not been out on a milk round since his hoof had been 'quicked' by the blacksmith's nail.

They were talking in lowered voices and I could not hear what they were saying. Uncle George went in to the stable while Dad looked on over the half door. He placed his arms on the top of the door and then leaned forward to rest his chin on them, watching whatever Uncle George was doing in the stable intently. After five minutes Uncle George emerged, closed the stable door behind him and the two of them continued their conversation. Dad turned away, stroking his chin in contemplation. He walked across the yard and then back again. He was slowly shaking his head. Whatever they were discussing, they seemed to be having difficulty making their mind up. I would have joined them but I did not want to move from my hiding place for fear of disturbing the swallows. I watched as Uncle George left the yard. Dad stood leaning on the stable door and although I could not make out what he was saying, I could hear him talking to Danny.

Uncle George reappeared but this time he was with Granddad and a man in a green boiler suit; I presumed he must be here 'on business'. I changed my position so that I had a better view of the yard. The four of them stood outside Danny's stable and now I could overhear enough to know that they were talking about his lameness. Then they moved on and walked towards the midden and the old stable where I lay concealed.

The boiler suit must have asked about the midden because I heard Granddad say that it did not leak as it was sealed with concrete. I never knew that. The midden was the one feature of the stable yard that did not attract much attention from me. Then I heard the boiler suit ask 'Who's Flush?' I knew the answer to that one. 'Flush' had been Dad's dog when he was a young man. Dad had told us many stories about growing up on the family farm and from those I knew that Flush had been his constant companion. The dog had died when Dad was home on leave from the army. Dad had said that even though he was a grown man by that time, he had still cried when Flush had died. He had buried his dog next to the midden and had carved the name 'FLUSH' in capital letters on one of the bricks in the midden wall. That is what must have caught the boiler suit's attention.

They moved into the old stable beneath me. Although they were closer, their voices were muffled by the wooden floor and the hay on which I was lying. I heard the words 'only used for storage now', and 'just needs weatherproofing', but I could not tell who said what. I concluded from this snatch of conversation that on this occasion, 'on business' meant engaging the boiler suit to do some repairs. They moved back into the yard and then turned out of my sight. A moment later I heard a low metallic boom as someone kicked their foot against the large aluminium tank in the water house; it was filled with gallons of cold water. Then their voices faded away and I deduced that they had gone through into the shippon.

I lay in the hay and thought about what repairs were needed. These were old buildings and probably needed a lot doing to them, but I liked them as they were. Eventually,

I heard the adults come out of the shippon and I watched as they walked out of the stable yard via the lean-to.

As I gazed out of the open hatch I could see the blue sky, crossed by the slowly melting white lines of aeroplane vapour trails. If I squinted, it looked like church music had been written in the sky. The late morning August sun was beating down and the hayloft was feeling warm and comfortable. I didn't normally fall asleep during the day – I was too old now for that sort of stuff. But I must have dozed off in the heat, because the next thing I was aware of was Dad calling me for dinner.

As I walked back to the house and entered the covered yard, I noticed the familiar smell of Nana's reheated Scouse. I joined Dad at the kitchen sink and washed my hands. We followed Nana inside; she was carrying a big pan. In the dining room we found Ann sitting at the table with Granddad. We all sat around the table while Nana dished each of us a plate of steaming Scouse. It was made with beef, lamb, potatoes, onions and carrots. 'Muck in!' Granddad announced, and we did.

I asked why it was called 'Scouse'. Dad said it came from the name 'Lobscouse', which was a sort of meat and potato stew eaten by sailors. Granddad said that Lobscouse was eaten by seamen who sailed into Liverpool from Norway, Holland and Germany. 'They made it from whatever was left over on the ship by the time they arrived in port,' he explained. He went on to say that Liverpool sailors became known as 'Scousers' and eventually it became a word used to describe anyone from Liverpool. Nana said that she had got the recipe from her mum.

When we had finished our Scouse dinner, Dad announced that the Corpy had been mowing the grass at Allerton Cemetery and had given us permission to go and rake some off for the horses. So he and Uncle George were taking Rupert and the milk van to the cemetery to load up. He asked Ann and me if we wanted to go along and help out and we both eagerly agreed. He said that he had to see someone 'on business' so Uncle George would take us up and he would follow on his bike. By the time we went back into the stable yard, Uncle George had Rupert hitched and ready to go. He was just loading the two large wooden hay rakes into the back of the van. We joined him in the van and Dad opened the gates for us to pull out. I noticed a large horsebox parked on the pavement just outside. I presumed that this belonged to whoever Dad was seeing 'on business'.

The sun was high in the sky and shining brightly. It was turning into a beautiful late summer's day. Uncle George kept Rupert at a slow walk as we lazily made our way down Duke Street and along James Street to begin the climb up Woolton Road. As we passed the war memorial, I recognised the vet's car travelling in the opposite direction.

'There's Mr Tomlinson,' I piped. 'He must be out doing his rounds.'

'Aye,' agreed Uncle George, in his usual monosyllabic manner.

We passed under the railway bridge and turned right as Woolton Road branched away from Mather Avenue. As we followed the dual carriageway Uncle George kept Rupert in the offside lane in preparation for the right-hand turn into the cemetery. Opposite the cemetery gates, the central reservation was cut by an access road and as we approached it Uncle George held the whip out through the right-hand doorway of the van to let traffic behind us know that we were intending to turn. There was no traffic on the other carriageway so we swung around and crossed it without stopping and then passed through the impressive gates of Allerton Cemetery.

I had travelled past the cemetery on many occasions but had never been through the gates. They reminded me of the gates to the Addams family mansion: black metalwork attached to tall sandstone gate posts. As we passed through the gateway it was like entering another world; a world of trees, hedgerows, perfectly manicured lawns and, of course, gravestones. There were gravestones in their thousands, rows upon rows of them in all shapes and sizes. And there was a peace about the place. Even the birds had stopped singing.

From between the two sandstone gatehouses, I could see the spires of three chapels peeping above the treetops. Running straight ahead of us was a wide tree-lined driveway, which formed the main route through the centre of the site. I could see why it had to be wide, as gliding towards us was a funeral cortège with half a dozen or so cars following each other, bumper to bumper. There were other cars parked at the side, but there was plenty of room for everyone to pass. The driveway was lined on either side by a long holly hedge growing in front of two parallel rows of horse chestnut trees. I would have made a mental note to return here in autumn to collect conkers, but I was too old now for that sort of stuff.

Rupert walked us around the central chapel, which formed a roundabout in the middle of the driveway. Further on we came to a second gateway. It was at this point that a well-wooded public footpath crossed the site, and as we passed between these gates and trundled over the footpath, we could see that we were now entering a newer part of the cemetery.

Uncle George pulled Rupert over to the left, where there was a narrower track at right angles to the main driveway. Here, next to the wooded footpath, lay a piece of land yet to be populated with gravestones. It looked like one huge lawn and we could see that it had recently been mown, with the cuttings left to lie. As we pulled onto the grass, its aroma wrapped itself around us. Ann and I filled our lungs with its rich sweetness. 'Ahhhhhhh,' we both exhaled, like the kids in the Bisto advert. There was something simply perfect about the smell of freshly cut grass on a hot, sunny, summer's day.

Uncle George tied the reins so that they would not fall through the front window, but would give Rupert enough head to enable the horse to graze at his leisure. He picked up the two hay rakes and walked over to the edge of the lawn where the rows of gravestones began. He leant one rake against the nearest gravestone and began working with the other. As we approached him, he nodded to the standing rake and said, 'You can try your hand at raking if you like.'

We wandered over to the gravestone on which the rake was leaning. Ann looked at the epitaph and read aloud: 'From thence he shall come to judge the quick and the dead.' I recognised that. 'It's from the Apostles' Creed,' I observed. As a choirboy there were certain parts of the church service that I knew by heart and the Apostles' Creed was one of these. Ann looked at me with a furrowed brow. She wasn't convinced. 'It is! It's the bit that goes like this,' I insisted, and began to recite from memory:

On the third day he rose from the dead;

He ascended into heaven,

And sitteth on the right hand of God,

The Father Almighty;

From thence he shall come,

To judge the quick and the dead.

Ann nodded her head in recognition. 'What's "the quick"?' She pondered. We both looked again at the inscription.

Although I had been saying these words every Sunday for many years, I suddenly realised that I did not fully understand their meaning. 'Erm, the sensitive part of a horse's hoof?' I offered.

'It means "the living",' said Uncle George, standing behind us. 'The living and the dead.' That made sense.

'What about a horse's hoof?' I asked him.

'The quick of the hoof is the living part of the hoof. All the rest is dead. That's why the horse can't feel anything there,' he explained. That also made perfect sense. Another piece in another puzzle.

Uncle George returned to his task. He raked the grass into a line using long sweeps of the rake. He worked with an easy rhythm that came from a lifetime of practice. Ann and I took it in turns to use the other rake but it was too big for us and we found it awkward. Very soon we were both sweating with the effort and we collapsed onto the small heap we had created. The smell of the grass was intoxicating and we both lay there, immersed in it, staring up at the blue heavens, trying to see shapes in the high clouds. The sky looked like 'the Creation' in the Children's

Illustrated Bible. Ann said she could see a dragon, a witch and Australia. I told her I could see a snowy owl, an arctic fox and Thunderbird 2.

Once we had sufficiently recovered from our short labours, we sat up and looked around. Rupert was casually grazing. He pulled the van around with him as he went. Uncle George was still silently raking, his swinging rhythm continuing without pause. He now had two straight lines of grass running the full length of the open site.

'He's like a robot,' whispered Ann.

'Danger, Will Robinson!' I laughed and threw a handful of grass at her.

Then, from the direction of the wooded footpath, I heard a familiar 'kor-kork' call. 'That's a pheasant!' I gushed. We picked ourselves up and scuttled over to the wooded area to investigate further. We moved into its shadow and the coolness was welcome. We stood on the edge and peered into the gloom. There was no sign of the pheasant but my attention was grabbed by one of my favourite wildflowers. I stooped to pick a green feathery leaf from the fern-like plant that had an umbrella of tiny white floral heads. I rolled the leaf between my palms and then held my cupped hands up to my nose. 'Mmmm, sweet cicely,' I purred. 'Smell this.' I offered it to Ann and she pushed her nose between my cupped thumbs and inhaled.

'Oh. Liquorice!' she announced in disbelief.

I laughed, delighting in her wonderment. 'It always reminds me of the liquorice sticks and aniseed balls in Hilda's sweet shop,' I said. She sniffed the leaves again and heartily agreed with me.

We took a few more steps along the woodland's edge and then Ann sat herself down on a nearby log and rolled down the ankle sock on her right leg. 'I've been stung by a nettle,' she said. I looked at her shin. There was a cluster of four or five white-headed spots where the nettle had stung her through her sock.

'I'll find you a dock leaf to rub on it,' I offered.

'That's just an old wives' tale.'

I assured her that I had used dock leaves before and that they really did work on nettle stings. She gave this some thought. In her face I could see her scepticism wrestling with her acknowledgement that her younger brother did know a thing or two about the natural world. My demonstration with the sweet cicely must have won out for, eventually, she consented. I set off in search of a broad-leaved dock. I did not have to look very far as nettles and docks always grow near to each other. I picked a large flat leaf and took it to Ann. I told her she had to rub it on to get the dock's juices into the stings. She did this and then I blew on the stings to cool them. After a few minutes she agreed that the pain had soothed. Ha! Maybe brothers aren't so bad after all, I thought to myself.

Just then the sight of a blue Hillman Imp pulling up on the driveway caught our attention. Dad and Granddad slowly climbed out and wandered over to us. Like Uncle George, even though it was a hot day, they both were wearing west-kuts over their rolled-up shirt sleeves. Dad said he had taken the opportunity to get in some driving practice rather than ride up on his bike. He spoke quietly, as if in respect for the dead. Then, he recovered the second rake and went to help Uncle George rake up the long lines of grass.

Ann showed Granddad her nettle stings and I eagerly told him about the dock leaf remedy. 'Aye,' he agreed. 'There's plenty of medicine and food growing in the wild. Let's see what else we can find.'

The three of us ambled along the woodland edge. Granddad pointed to a small, delicate-looking plant with clusters of tiny white florets sitting on an upright green stalk, standing about ten inches high. There were lots of these dotted around the woodland floor. 'That's pignut,' he said. 'When I was a lad we used to go digging up pignuts for a treat.' He explained that at the bottom of the roots of this plant was an edible nut. He took a penknife from the pocket of his westkut, bent down and began to dig away at the roots of the plant. As he dug, he told us that pigs used to dig up the nuts and that was why they were now called pignuts.

When his knife reached the nutty prize at the end of the roots, he dug it out and wiped it with his handkerchief. He told us that it needed to be peeled and washed before it could be eaten. 'It's also known as St Anthony's Nut,' he said, as he gave it to Ann.

His favouritism was predictable but it still irked me. Maybe Ann sensed this for, after examining the grubby nut, she looked at me and said, 'If it's named after St Anthony, then you should have it.' She offered it to me and I accepted it gratefully. Maybe sisters aren't so bad after all, I thought to myself.

I asked who St Anthony was and why the nut was named after him. Granddad said that there was more than one St Anthony but that he did not know why the nut was so named. 'Maybe it's because all Anthonys go a little bit nuts at times,' I suggested. Granddad managed a smile. I put the nut in my pocket.

We walked on some more until Granddad stopped next to a damp area and pointed at a thick clump of large wavy-edged, lance-shaped leaves from which erupted a long bristly stem topped by a bell-shaped cluster of purple, violet, white and yellow flowers. 'Ah. That's comfrey,' he said. 'Its grand stuff. We used to use that as a poultice to cure all sorts of problems with horses' legs and feet.'

'Would it cure a quicked hoof?' I chirped.

Granddad looked at me blankly. I was about to repeat my question when Dad called for us to come and help load the van. He and Uncle George had raked the grass into large heaps dotted about the site. We ran over and began picking up armfuls of grass from the heaps and carrying them to the van. This was so much fun and as we worked Ann and I giggled away to each other. The three adults went about their work in more sombre fashion; maybe it's because we're in a cemetery, I thought.

It felt good to be working out in a field with the rest of the family. I imagined that this is how it had been for Dad when he was a lad. With all five of us working together, we soon had the back of the van piled high. Uncle George put a couple of sack cloths on the top of the pile to prevent the grass from blowing away once we were on the road. Ann and I offered to sit on the sacks to help keep everything pressed down. But before we left, I ran back to the woodland edge to pick one more leaf of sweet cicely.

Dad and Granddad set off in the car ahead of us, and Uncle George allowed Rupert to walk all the way back to the dairy. We travelled back in silence, listening to the steady clip-clop of Rupert's hooves. I crushed the sweet cicely leaf between the palms of my hands and Ann and I took it in turns to inhale the liquorice-aniseed fragrance. It was a lovely lazy journey. I would have wanted it to last forever, except that by the time we passed under the railway bridge at Allerton station, I was bursting for a pizz.

When we arrived back at the dairy, Dad and Granddad were waiting for us. Uncle George pulled Rupert into the stable yard. As Ann and I dismounted from the van, Dad and Granddad approached us and said they had something to tell us. I made a beeline for the toilet. 'I'm just goin' to the lavvy,' I called over my shoulder. 'I'll be back in a mo.'

After the blissful relief of emptying a full bladder, I went into the kitchen to wash my hands. There was no sign of Nana. On my way back to the stable yard I met Ann and Granddad. He had his arm around her shoulder and she was crying. After such an enjoyable afternoon I was shocked to see this. 'What's the matter?' I asked. Granddad told me to go and see Dad in the yard and he would explain. Puzzled, I watched as the two of them walked up the whitewashed passageway to the house and then I went in search of Dad.

As I walked into the stable yard, Uncle George was leading Rupert back into the shippon. Dad had just closed the gates to the yard and was about to start unloading the grass, but he stopped when he saw me.

'What's the matter with Ann?' I asked him.

'Come and sit down here,' he said, indicating the step of the van. 'I've a bit of sad news for you.'

I sat on the step and he bent down in front of me with his hands on his thighs and tried to look me straight in the eye. There was no sign of the usual humour in his face, just a look of resignation, with a hint of concern. 'It's about Danny. I'm afraid the infection in his foot spread and we had to have him put down.'

That took a moment to register. I suppressed the natural instinct to ask him to repeat his statement. Instead, I stared at him while I ran through it again in my head. He was saying that Danny was dead – past tense. It had already happened. There was nothing I could do. I was dumbstruck. It was only a couple of weeks since he first went lame and I thought he had been getting better. Then, many other questions galloped into my head like the six honest serving-men on horseback: What and Why and When and How and Where and Who? I cleared my head and then I thought about my sister. 'Is that why Ann was crying?'

'Yes. She's upset.' He looked at me closely and put his hand on my shoulder. 'How are you feeling?'

How was I feeling? I didn't know. How was I supposed to feel? Danny had always been there. I could just about recollect being small enough to be able to walk under his belly without bending. But he was a horse, not a person. I thought about Great Auntie Flora. I hadn't cried when she died earlier in the year, so it didn't seem right to cry now. I thought about Dad and how he had said he had cried when Flush had died.

'I feel – sad,' I said with care. 'But, I'm not going to cry.'

'Okay.'

'How are you feeling?' I asked him.

'Me?' My question took him by surprise. After a moment's hesitation he said, 'I feel sad too, but I'm not going to cry either.'

Then the questions began to flow. I asked him when this had happened. He said Mr Tomlinson had come while we were at the cemetery and the van from the 'knackers' yard had been here to take Danny away. The trip to the cemetery, Mr Tomlinson on his rounds, the horsebox parked outside – all pieces, slotting into the jigsaw. Then I remembered about Uncle George and Dad talking in the yard that morning, about how quiet the adults had been at the cemetery and about the look on Granddad's face when I had asked about treating a quicked hoof – more pieces in the jigsaw.

I asked why Danny had had to be put down. Dad said that the infection in the quick of the hoof had spread; it was preventing Danny from walking and it had reached a point where it was poisoning his blood. He explained that because Danny was so old, his body was unable to fight the infection. Putting him down had been the kindest thing to do.

'He had a long life and a good one; a long working life,' mused Dad. 'But, when people get too old, it's time to stop.'

'People?' I queried.

'Erm, horses,' he corrected. 'When horses get too old, it's time to stop.'

I asked how Danny had been put down. He explained that Mr Tomlinson had used something called a 'Greener Humane Killer', which fires a captive bolt into the animal's brain, killing it instantly. He said that it was a quick end and that Danny would not have suffered. 'The quick and the dead', I thought to myself, but I sensed that this was not the appropriate time for humour. And, although I was curious to know more, I sensed that this was not the appropriate time for detail, either.

Dad saw me looking past him at Danny's stable. 'Do you want to have a look inside?' he asked. I nodded. We went over to the stable and Dad opened the top door. We leant on the bottom door and peered inside.

Of course, the stable was empty. Danny had gone. But his heat was still in there. I closed my eyes and I could clearly picture him standing in his stall and I could hear the sound he made as he munched his oats. I breathed in deeply through my nose and I could still smell him. The two of us stood there in silence, each with our own thoughts.

After a while I turned away and Dad closed the stable door. Just then Ann came back into the yard and walked over to me. Her eyes were red and her cheeks were stained where her tears had run. 'Do you know?' She managed to ask me.

'Yeah,' I replied and then she began to cry again. I stepped towards her and put her head on to my shoulder and we hugged each other. Then Dad put his arms around us both and the three of us stood there in the yard. Dad smelled of horse, of Danny. But his embrace was soothing – like a comfrey poultice on a weeping wound.

Chapter Fifteen

JACOB'S LADDER

I could always count on the Duke Street Kids to cheer me up. We had gathered together to play in the shippon as it had been raining off and on. It wasn't just ordinary rain. Lightning and rolling thunder punctuated the showers. It was the sort of muggy weather where you can taste the electricity in the air. Dad said it was nature's way of letting us know that summer was coming to an end.

The shippon not only offered us shelter from the rain but also provided us with our very own rustic playground. At one end it housed a number of stalls; the horses, Peggy and Rupert, occupied two of these. Another was occupied by Uncle George's henhouse. He had eight chickens: seven hens and one cockerel. We had christened the latter 'Hennery The Eighth'. The chickens had the free run of the whole of the shippon and would often find their way out into the yard, even when the shippon doors were closed; they seemed to know every nook and cranny. At the other end was what looked like a graveyard for agricultural implements.

Bits and pieces of rusting metal, shaped timber structures and miscellaneous harness occupied every available square foot of floor and wall.

In the central part of the shippon was a large area of flat staging made of wooden pallets. Upon this staging were stored bales of hay and straw. The hay was used to feed the horses and the straw was used for bedding. On a fairly regular basis throughout the year there would be deliveries of new bales. These were stacked in a crude pyramid, which, on occasions, could be up to ten bales high. For us kids, the bales were like a giant Lego set. As well as racing, climbing, jumping and hiding in the hay, the odd hay fight was also an option. When we were younger we used to build dens – but we were too old now for that sort of stuff.

Fixed to the shippon wall behind the haystack was a wooden ladder. We called it 'Jacob's Ladder' after the story in the Children's Illustrated Bible. It went straight up to the shippon ceiling where there was an open square hatch. It then disappeared into the darkness of the roof space beyond. We did not know what lay up there. We were pretty sure it was not Heaven and we knew without doubt that we were not little angels, but we called it 'Jacob's Ladder' anyway. The ceiling was the equivalent of two storeys high and one of the challenges we set ourselves was to see who could jump off the highest rung on to the hay below. Each time we tried it someone would go one more rung higher than anyone had gone before.

We had just finished arranging the hay so that we had a layer of tied bales on the edge of the pallet staging. This was then covered by a couple of broken bales. Through trial and error we had found this to be the safest combination. You had to jump out from the ladder a couple of feet in order to land on the hay, otherwise it was the cold stone floor of the shippon and that was not worth thinking about. Being two years older than the rest of us, Bonzo and Uncle Robert had a physical advantage but we were determined to beat them whenever we could. Jacob's Ladder wasn't just about physical strength; it was also about nerve – and we had bucketfuls of that.

Once you were as high as you dared go, you would carefully turn yourself around, concentrate on the spot you wanted to hit and then launch yourself into space, singing or shouting your signature tune. Quite early on you learned to roll when you hit the hay otherwise your chin would make contact with your knee and a chipped tooth or a lacerated lip would be the outcome. You also learned to roll in the direction of the haystack rather than the stone floor. We could count twenty rungs before the ladder disappeared beyond the ceiling. All of us had previously conquered ten rungs of the ladder. It was quite dizzying, looking down from that height.

I was not particularly comfortable with heights but seeing as this was 'my land' (to quote Jacob), I felt obliged to push the limit. I stood at the bottom of the ladder and looked up. The hatch seemed so far above. I began to climb. The rungs were not round, like those on a window cleaner's ladder; they were more like rectangular blocks. This meant that you could not make a fist and grip them between your thumb and fingers. You just had to hook your fingers over the upper edge and hang on like some kind of four-toed tree sloth.

The Duke Street Kids counted me up to twelve rungs. I managed to keep my fear under control but I held on to the ladder so tight that my knuckles were white. When I inched my way around and looked down, I could see six faces looking up at me. They seemed so far below. I looked around at the shippon and was struck by how different the world appeared when you changed your perspective. The voices from below urged me on. I chose my spot and with an ever so slightly nervous 'Der-Derrrr, Der-Der,' from my *Stingray* signature tune, I jumped from the ladder. Those seconds of freefall were exhilarating. I hit the hay and rolled towards the stack. The impact jarred my body but I was too excited for it to bother me. The cheer I received was almost as exhilarating as the freefall.

However, my triumph seemed set to be short-lived as Uncle Robert announced he would do fifteen rungs. We all watched as he rearranged the hay and then began to climb. After twelve rungs he slowed down and began placing both feet on a rung before stepping up to the next. He was holding himself very close to the ladder. We all counted aloud the number of the rung he had reached. At the fifteenth rung we gave a little cheer but we could sense his discomfort.

When he didn't begin turning himself for the jump, Bonzo asked, 'Are you okay, Bob?' That gave an added air of seriousness to the situation, as we had never heard Bonzo refer to him by any name other than 'Uncle Robert'. He didn't answer. Bonzo asked him again.

'Wait a minute,' he replied in a very thin voice that was hardly recognisable as Uncle Robert's. We craned our necks and waited in silence. After a hundred heartbeats he began to move. He carefully shuffled his feet so that he was facing away from the wall of the shippon. His jump was not the usual whooping leap of excitement we all had experienced. It was hesitant and begrudging and there was no attempt at a signature tune. As he dropped like a silent stone, his body seemed uncoordinated and he didn't wave his arms to keep his balance. He hit the hay without rolling and for a moment he disappeared. His impact had snapped the hairy twine that bound the bale and it had collapsed under him. Before we could reach him he jumped out of his hole, staggered to the wall and threw up. When he eventually looked up at us, his face was the colour of a Dolly Blue wash.

'Well done, Bob,' said Bonzo quietly.

'Thanks,' Uncle Robert replied, quite subdued. 'I'm not feeling too good.'

'That's the highest anyone has jumped,' announced Trebor. 'You've got the record Uncle Robert – unless Bonzo can beat you?'

We all turned to Bonzo. He looked at us, looked at Uncle Robert and then looked up at the ladder. He didn't say anything. He threw a fresh bale into the hole made by Uncle Robert, walked over to the ladder and began to climb. We started to count. When he reached the fifteenth rung he paused and then took another step up.

'Sixteen!' We cheered.

He took another step up and this time there was silence. He kept on climbing until his head was just below the ceiling level. He took another, slower step up and his head disappeared into the square hatch. At that moment there was an explosion of thunder directly above us. It was so loud we could feel it through the stone floor. Even Bonzo flinched and then a fine rain of dust began to descend from the shippon ceiling.

'Shee-it!' Shithead swore. 'That scared the fuggin' life out of me!' There was a ripple of nervous laughter that passed as we concentrated once more on what Bonzo was doing. We could see from his body movements that he was having a look around at whatever lay beyond the ceiling.

This time Falco broke the silence. 'Is it heaven?' He called up.

We laughed again. Bonzo looked down at us and grinned. Then in a very matter-of-fact way, he descended to the fifteenth rung, turned and jumped. He hit the hay and rolled almost straight into a standing position. A marvellous execution. He walked over to Uncle Robert, patted him on the back and said, 'Sorry mate, we'll just have to share the record for now.'

Not fully appreciating the magnanimity of this gesture, we eagerly quizzed him about what was beyond the ceiling. He told us it was an empty roof space illuminated by a large skylight with nothing up there but a couple of dead pigeons and loads of cobwebs. Also, he said that the ceiling seemed paper thin and so there was no way you could walk on it. This was far short of what our lively imaginations had led us to believe might be up there. What a disappointment.

Uncle Robert had sat down on the hay bales and we moved to join him. Trebor jumped down from the stack and landed on the bales on the seat of his pants. 'The Eagle has landed,' he announced.

'The Eagle has landed,' mimicked Tubs, and then farted. We fell about laughing. 'Imagine - warrit'd be like – if Neil

Armstrong – apple tarted in his spacesuit,' he spluttered out between gulps of air. This did nothing to help anyone get his breath back; we laughed ourselves silly.

'Will someone jump on his head?' begged Trebor.

No one did, but eventually, calm descended on us. 'How do they do that in space? Yer know? How do they go to the bog in a spacecraft?' mused Falco. 'How do you stop it just floating around in the spaceship?' Probably because we were just too tired to laugh any more, this question was taken seriously.

'We did it as a project in school,' said Uncle Robert, with some colour returning to his cheeks.

'What? Yer had to pizz in space?' Falco quizzed him.

'No, yer divvy,' snorted Uncle Robert as he threw a handful of hay at Falco. 'We did a project on the moon landing. They asked American school kids to send in questions and that was the most asked question.'

'Yeah,' confirmed Bonzo. 'They have to pizz into a tube.'

'Cumoffit,' scoffed Falco, in disbelief.

'Yous are Tom Pepperin' us,' accused Trebor.

'No, really,' assured Uncle Robert. 'It works like a vacuum cleaner, so that nuffin' gets leaked.'

'Urgh! Imagine pizzin' into the vacuum cleaner at home. Yer mar would go spare!' said Trebor. That got a laugh. We were beginning to recover.

'Then they press a button and it gets squirted out into space,' Bonzo continued. 'Then it freezes into water crystals.'

'So, are yer saying that Neil Armstrong's pizz is still orbiting the earth?' I said.

'Errm, could be, I s'pose,' shrugged Bonzo.

'Either that, or it rains down on us,' observed Uncle Robert.

We gave that some thought. Outside, there was a particularly heavy shower. I could hear the rain, rumbling against the shippon roof and the conversation created a picture in my mind of the Apollo 11 astronauts flying overhead and pizzin' down on us from their spaceship. Then Bonzo broke the reverie.

'Speaking of which, I need to take a pizz,' he announced.

'What? Are yer going for another record?' Trebor joked.

This was a reference to the fact that Bonzo was the only one of us who had so far been able to pizz over the midden wall. Many a time there would be the seven of us lined up, facing the wall, competing to see who could pizz the highest. Being the tallest, Bonzo had a definite advantage.

'Oh yeah, sure,' Bonzo laughed. 'Yesterday the midden wall, tomorrow the Berlin Wall!' He walked over to the shippon gates and pulled them open. 'Flippin' 'eck! Its rainin' pickhandles! Where can I go without getting soaked?'

'Use the stalls,' I suggested, pointing over to where Rupert and Peggy were tied up.

'I'm not pizzin' next to a flippin' horse!'

'He can't stand the competition!' Falco jibed.

'I need to go too,' said Uncle Robert.

'Right. Your house is nearest. Let's leg it there,' decided Bonzo.

And with that, the two honorary members of the gang left us at a gallop. I closed the shippon doors behind them and rejoined the lads on the hay bales. The conversation moved back to Jacob's Ladder and each of us described what we had thought would be up in the loft.

Eventually, we could hear that the rain had stopped, so we went out into the yard. The sky above us was still the colour of bathwater and you could tell that the storm hadn't finished with us just yet. I loved the way everything smelled fresh after heavy rain but as I breathed in deeply, there was just a hint of something not so fresh. I scanned the yard, turning towards the open gates, and there, standing to one side, leaning against the gatepost, was Steven Scales. There was another growl of thunder.

He always reeked of cigarettes and he was smoking now. I realised it was that which had soured the air. 'Where's Bonzo?' Scales asked.

Good, I thought, if he's after Bonzo, he will go away and look for him.

'He's gone round to Uncle Robert's,' replied Tubs, looking important.

That smarmy smile told me that if we wanted Scales to move on, then that was the wrong answer. He was not looking to find Bonzo; he was looking to avoid him. And now he knew that Bonzo was not here.

'Okay if I come in then?' He walked uninvited into the yard.

I could feel the panic welling up inside me as my body prepared itself to run like the wind. I looked for an escape route, but with the van in the yard there was little room for manoeuvre. As he advanced, my exits closed and I could see on his face that he knew it. He had us trapped, snookered, well and truly Joe Palookad. I looked at the others, my eyes pleading for any crumb of support. But they were all looking at me. My stomach was a swarm of cowardy-custard cabbage whites. I swallowed hard but my mouth was as dry as a dandy brush. Here we go again – and, this time with an audience of my closest friends.

I prayed for Dad to appear or for Bonzo to come back – anything. I hated being scared but I did not know any other way to be. All I had to do was say 'No,' but I knew I was going to say 'Okay'. I wanted to resist my fear. I wanted to stand my ground. Like Jacob, this was my land; my family's land. I didn't want him anywhere near it or my family. I didn't want him anywhere near me. I hated him. I could smell him. He stank of evil; I guess I stank of fear.

'No,' I half whispered. Oh shit.

'Wha?' Arrogant disbelief.

'We're just going,' I lied.

'Yer horse died, didn't it?' he taunted.

Bastard. My breathing quickened. My heart thumped. My knees shook. I readied myself to run. What the hell was Danny to do with him? Bastard. My fists clenched. He pulled on his cigarette and blew smoke into the air with a cocky laugh. I grasped at that. 'Yer can't come in here smoking,' I insisted.

He stopped laughing. 'I'll burn the rest of yer fuggin' horses if I want,' he threatened. 'You gonna stop me?'

Run! Run! Run! Run!

'Yeah.' Oh SHIT!

'I'd like to see yer fuggin' try.' With that he stepped towards me.

Run now! Run now! Now! Now! NOW! The thunder exploded in my head.

I hit him.

I hit him once – but I hit him with everything I had. I hit him with a body that could lift milk crates and ride the Death Steps. I hit him with a stubbornness that could conquer The Beast and climb Jacob's Ladder. I hit him with all of my fear. I hit him with all of my shame. I hit him with years of running away. And I hit him for Danny.

He hit the floor.

He saw my unpractised punch coming and he tried to duck. But I was fast – as fast as the lightning. My right fist connected with the side of his head. He staggered. Then his knees buckled and his hips folded. He collapsed in sections and then hit the floor. He tried to get up but he couldn't. He sprawled like you do after you have been spinning and then lie down and can't get up because although you have stopped, the world is still going around.

I did not know what to do next. I did not know what was expected of me. Should I run now or should I hit him again? I stepped forward and scrunched out his cigarette where it had fallen on the cobbled floor of the yard.

He pulled himself up on the side of the van. Somehow, he did not seem to be as tall now. 'I'll fuggin' kill yew!' he spat at me.

'No yer fuggin' won't,' came a voice from behind me – it was Tubs.

'Gerron yer fuggin' way, Scales,' added Trebor.

My four friends stepped forward to stand next to me, two either side. Scales took in the sight of the five of us. 'I'll get the fuggin' lorra yers,' he threatened as he backed off towards the gates.

'Yeah, go and tell Bonzo all about it,' taunted Shithead.

'And Uncle Robert,' added Falco.

'Likkle bastiids!' he cursed, as he turned and left the yard.

We looked at each other. 'Shee-it,' exhaled Shithead after a moment.

'Well done, Deejay,' said Tubs, quietly.

'Yeah, well done, Deejay,' repeated Trebor.

'It's about time someone did that to Scales,' said Falco.

'I think I've broken my berloody fist,' I winced. And with that we all laughed. It was a nervous but excited sort of laughter. I felt like I was going to be sick but I was determined not to lose my newfound face by throwing up in front of everyone, like Uncle Robert had done.

'Are yer okay?' Shithead said. 'Yer look like shit.'

'Yeah,' I lied. 'Let's go back in and sit down.'

We returned to the shippon and sat on the hay bales. The four of them jabbered on about fighting but I wasn't fully paying attention. The pain in my right arm was growing. It was a kind of pain I'd never experienced before. Not the red pain of cuts and grazes and not the blue pain of recirculation, but something in between. I could not rid myself of this new, purple pain. Gradually, it wore down my resistance and after half an hour it was becoming unbearable. I told the lads that I was going to go in and put a cold flannel on my arm. They accepted this without question, complaint or criticism. We left the shippon. The four of them walked off down Duke Street and I walked towards the dairy.

As I crossed the jigger I could no longer hold back the tears; at least none of the lads had seen me cry, though. I didn't want any of the adults to know I had been fighting but I struggled to think of a believable explanation for my condition. I climbed the stone steps into the kitchen, nursing my right arm. Both Nana and Granddad were in the kitchen. I told them I had hurt my arm. They asked me how I did it but when I sobbed instead of answering, they focused on my injury. Nana soaked a flannel under the tap and placed it on my wrist.

'What did you do?' Granddad asked again.

I was in too much discomfort to think of a lie. 'I hit Steven Scales,' I admitted.

'Did you now?' he enquired. 'And why do that?'

'He was smoking and was going to set fire to the stables.'

'And so you hit him, eh? And what happened then?'

Might as well come clean and get it all out of the way, I thought. 'He fell down. I think I knocked him out.'

They looked at each other. There was a moment's silence and then, 'Good for you,' nodded Nana as she busied herself removing the flannel to give it another soak.

The constant reapplication of coldness did help with the pain but it was obvious there was something wrong. About an hour later Mum called in at the dairy. She had been shopping in the village. 'Lord help us! In the wars again!' She declared. After examining my wrist she decided to take me to Garston Hospital to be on the safe side. It was literally around the corner, at the end of James Street. It was officially called The Alfred Jones Memorial Hospital and it stood atop its own sandstone outcrop overlooking Woolton Road. I did not know Alfred Jones, but Dad had told me that he was a rich businessman who was very ill one morning and decided to donate money for a new hospital; unfortunately he died that same day. I imagined he must have been very rich because the hospital building looked like a millionaire's mansion – like Wayne Manor in the *Batman* TV series. Dad had said that it was built in 1916, just in time to treat four hundred and sixty-five soldiers who were wounded in the war.

We knew the hospital well because once a month, after evensong, the choir would troupe across the village and sing a short service in one of the wards; it always smelled of ether and antiseptic. They did not have a full A&E department any more but they still dealt with minor casualties. Fortunately for me, they still had an X-ray machine.

The rain had stopped by the time Mum and I were walking up the long flight of twenty-six steps cut into the steep slope at the front of the building. Half way up she stopped for a breather. 'Blimey-daze,' she said, 'it's like bloomin' Jacob's Ladder.' Despite my discomfort, that made me smile; I didn't mention the shippon though.

We went to the reception desk. We waited. Then we went to the waiting room. We waited. Then we were seen by a nurse. She recommended an X-ray. We waited some more. I went into the X-ray theatre and had an X-ray. Then we waited some more. Eventually, my name was called and we went in to see a doctor. He was looking at my X-ray as we went in. He indicated for us to be seated.

'Well now,' he said. 'How did you hurt your wrist?'

'I punched Steven Scales,' I replied without further prompting. Mum tutted.

'Steven Scales, eh?' He glanced at Mum knowingly. 'Well – good for you,' he whispered and winked at me. 'Where did you hit him?'

'In the stable yard.'

'No, I mean where on his body did you hit him.'

'In the head,' I said, indicating the side of my cranium with my fist and then wincing at the pain caused by this movement.

'Ah. That explains it then.'

'Explains what?' Mum said.

'Explains how you come to have a broken wrist.'

'Oh, no,' Mum wailed. 'Well, let this be a lesson to you.

You should not be punching people in the head.'

'That's absolutely right,' agreed the doctor. 'The skull is designed to protect the brain. If you hit someone there you could do serious damage.' Then, in a more conspiratorial tone, he said, 'Next time, hit him on the jaw – that's much softer than the skull and you've less chance of damaging your hand.'

I was fitted with a metal splint. It was bandaged to the underside of my forearm and curled around into the palm of my hand. The doctor said I would have to wear it for at least three weeks.

'Three weeks!' I complained. 'That long? That's how long the Apollo astronauts stayed in quarantine for.' He laughed at that but confirmed that was how long it would take for the bone to set.

We left the building and started back down the twenty-six steps. Mum took her time while I bounced ahead.

'Slow down,' she called. 'You don't want to go hurting your hand again.'

I could not see how anything was going to hurt my hand with that metal splint in place; it looked like a piece of armour. I wondered if any of the four hundred and sixty-five soldiers wounded in the war had had a metal splint fitted.

I waited at the bottom of the steps for her. Before she reached me she stopped to rest. 'Me bloomin' knees!' she complained. Then she turned herself around and holding on to the hand rail, came down the last few steps backwards. She reached the bottom and I announced: 'One small step for Mum, one giant leap for mumkind!'

'Cheeky monkey!' she scolded and gave me a mock clip round the ear. We both laughed.

Chapter Sixteen

AT LOGGERHEADS

There was change in the air. When the thunderstorm had rolled its way up the Mersey and headed inland through the Cheshire Gap, it carried with it the mugginess of the summer and left in its wake a breezy freshness that smelled of the Irish Sea with just a hint of the wilder Atlantic Ocean beyond. High above, the north-westerly wind pushed billowing white clouds across the royal-blue sky like tall ships leaving the port in full sail, while down on the ground it rushed through the trees, testing the resolve of every tiring leaf and semi-ripened seed.

While I had been busy counting down the days until my splint would be removed, I had completely forgotten that Dad had a countdown of his own. Four weeks had passed since he announced to us that he would be taking his driving test, but he hadn't mentioned it since and we all had forgotten about it. The day of his test arrived and still he did not mention it. He just came home from the dairy one Monday evening, driving the car rather than riding his bike. He would normally come in through the back gate and park his bike in the blue asbestos shed in the back yard. But today he entered the house through the front door.

The three of us were sitting in front of the television. Billy was watching *The Magic Roundabout*. Ann and I were too old now for that sort of stuff – but we were watching it anyway. There was a commotion in the hall so we ran out to investigate. Dad was standing there with his 'L' plates in his hand and a grin that was so wide, it made his ears glow.

'Your dad's passed his driving test,' Mum announced with great enthusiasm.

'Wow! Erm ... what does that mean now, then?' I asked.

'It means I can drive the car on my own, without your granddad having to sit in with me,' explained Dad.

'It means we can go wherever we want, whenever we want,' enthused Mum. The whole family trooped outside to look at the car. It was parked on Garston Old Road, at the end of our front path. It was the only car parked on our block.

Both Mum and Dad were glowing with pride and gushing with excitement at our family's newly acquired status. As if to underline that point, Mum suggested that we take a quick ride around the park. Dad agreed to this. He opened the front passenger door and pushed the seat forward so that the three of us could climb into the back seat. Then he stood at the door to let Mum into the passenger seat. 'Your carriage awaits, milady,' he announced as she stepped inside. 'Lady Muck,' he sniggered before closing the door and we all laughed.

A spin around the park took us a matter of minutes. It was amazing how much Mum knew about driving. Although she had never sat behind a steering wheel in her life, she was full of helpful hints and advice for Dad:

'Not too fast.'

'Mind that child.'

'Not too close.'

'There's something coming.'

'You're alright now.'

Dad obviously appreciated this and listened intently without saying a single word until we were back in the house. But driving the new car was the only topic of conversation over tea (we had Heinz spaghetti on toast). As Mum seemed to know so much about driving, I asked if she was going to take a test also.

'Heavens above, no,' she replied. 'I'm not mechanically minded. Besides, if Dad drives me everywhere, there's no need for me to learn, is there, Eck?'

'Err, let me put it this way. If you want to get behind the wheel, I won't stand in your way,' he smirked. Mum gave him a quizzical look so he moved the conversation on quickly and told us about his test and the intricacies of his 'three-point turn', of his 'emergency stop' and his 'corner reversing'. He said that the only people he had told about taking his test were Mum and Granddad, because he didn't want to disappoint anyone if he failed.

'Are you going to use it to travel to the dairy?' I said.

'No,' he replied. 'It's not economical to use it for short journeys. For the time being I'll continue to use me bike to get to work. Either that or Shanks' pony.'

'Are we getting a pony?' Billy enquired. I suspected he wanted a pony to replace Danny, but I decided not to comment in case I upset him and incurred the wrath of Mum.

'No,' laughed Dad. 'Your "shanks" are part of your leg and "Shanks' pony" means "walking". I'll either walk or ride my bike to the dairy.'

'Where's your bike now?' Ann said.

'The Imp isn't big enough to fit my bike inside so I've left it at the dairy for now. I'll walk down after tea and pick it up.'

'What's the point in having a car if we're going to walk and cycle everywhere?' I asked.

'Oh, we're not going to walk and cycle everywhere,' replied Mum. 'There will be so much more we can do with a car and we can go to places we haven't been to before.'

'Like what?' I probed. Mum had hinted at this before but we had never talked about it in any detail.

'Well, for a start, we can drive to church, can't we, Eck?'

'Erm, well, we can when it's raining, I suppose,' replied Dad as he slurped a forkful of spaghetti into his mouth.

'And we can drive to Blackpool for our holidays next year,' Mum continued. Dad nearly choked on his spaghetti. 'Well, we can, can't we?' She insisted.

Dad swallowed and caught his breath. 'Aye. Once I've sorted the route out, I'm sure we can,' he said, winking at me. His gesture stopped me from mentioning God's own country – perhaps this was not the time.

'And we can go out for trips at the weekend,' she continued.

'How will we do that if me dad's working on Saturdays and we have to go to church on Sundays?' I argued. Dad snorted his agreement as he took another mouthful of spaghetti.

Mum pursed her lips impatiently. 'We don't have to go to church twice every Sunday,' she pointed out. 'If we go to matins we can simply tell the vicar that you won't be there for evensong.'

'Really? Wow!' I was astonished. Mum saying we didn't have to go to church was totally new territory.

'Yes,' she confirmed, looking very pleased with her logic. Clearly inspired, she continued. 'In fact, thinking about it, as there's nothing special on at church, we can do it this coming Sunday. Can't we, Eck?'

'Aye, I suppose so,' Dad conceded.

'Where are we going to go to?' I enthused.

'Well, where do you want to go to?' Mum asked of me.

I sensed an opportunity here. In her excitement, Mum seemed to have abandoned her usual stance of 'children should be seen and not heard' and, for once, had handed the initiative to me. I had to think quickly or that initiative would be lost. The Dales was the first place that came to mind but I knew instinctively that it would be rejected outright as it would be too far. It had to be somewhere challenging but realistic. Then I had it. 'Loggerheads!' I announced.

This time Dad did choke on his spaghetti. Mum had to slap him on his back to stop him coughing. Once recovered, he put his elbow on the table and rested his forehead in his hand. 'Berloody 'ell,' he laughed. 'I thought you were going to suggest Clarke Gardens or somewhere local like that. Why Loggerheads of all places?'

I reminded him that I had been there once before on a school trip to the Colomendy Field Studies Centre. I said that it was a great place to go for walks along the River Alyn or to climb the hills for fantastic views or sit and have a picnic at the tea gardens.

I sensed that my suggestion had the potential to bounce between them like a Wham-O Super Ball in a jigger. I decided to busy myself with my spaghetti and leave them to it.

'That sounds lovely,' said Mum. 'Let's do that, then.'

'It's in North Wales!' Dad spluttered. Mum met this with a blank expression. 'It's about fifty miles away and it'll take us over an hour to get there,' he explained.

'Well, we can do that, can't we?' She argued.

'Aye,' he sighed. 'I suppose we can. We could cross the Runcorn Bridge, bypass Chester and then go through Mold, I guess.'

'Right. That's settled then. And we can take our Amy and Mark with us as well.'

'What! And where the hell are they going to sit? It's a Hillman Imp, not a ruddy charabanc.'

'Mark can sit on Amy's knee and Billy can sit on my knee. It won't affect you. You'll be driving. That'll work, won't it?'

Dad must have been reading the signs and had decided that it was time to bow out gracefully. 'Alright,' he groaned as he rolled his eyes to the heavens in submission. 'We can always put someone in the boot.'

'We won't have to do that, you daft old man.'

'I'm not old,' he laughed.

That was how our first car trip to the countryside came about. Mum saw Aunty Amy on Friday at Garston Market and arranged for us to collect her and our cousin, Mark, from our grandma's house in Woolton. On Saturday she went to Winney Inch's hairdressers and splashed out on a new perm, especially for the occasion. Then, on Sunday, after matins, she spoke to the vicar and to Mr Moore, the choirmaster, and informed them that the Joy family would be absent from evensong as we would be taking a trip to North Wales in our new car (she omitted to mention that it was a second-hand car).

We finished Sunday lunch and then, before getting into the car, Mum insisted that we all try to go to the toilet, even if we didn't feel like it. 'We don't want to have to stop on the way there,' she explained.

Once Ann, Billy and I had all pretended to go to the toilet, we climbed into the back seat of the car and Mum sat herself in the front passenger seat. Dad brought out three folding garden chairs and a shopping bag containing cups and saucers, tea and coffee and two large thermos flasks; one filled with boiling water and the other containing cold milk. He put all of these into the boot of the Imp. Unlike any other car I had ever seen, the Hillman Imp had its engine at the back and its boot at the front. Once the boot was filled, we were ready to go.

It was strange travelling up Woolton Road in a car. Compared to what it was like being pulled by a horse, the scenery just flashed by. And whereas the horse would vary its pace according to the slope, the car maintained a constant speed going up or down hill. We completed the journey to Woolton in a matter of minutes – a journey it would have taken a horse much longer to make.

Under Mum's watchful eye and her continuous stream of helpful advice on how to drive, Dad managed to get us all to Grandma's house without killing anyone.

Grandma and Granddad were Mum's mum and dad. They lived at No. 37 Garway, in Woolton. This was the house Mum had grown up in after they moved from the 'tennies'. It had three storeys, with just about enough bedroom space to house a family of thirteen.

When we arrived, we all piled out of the car to pop indoors to say 'hello' to Grandma and Granddad. Aunty Amy and

Mark were also there, waiting for us. Mum usually talked for ages when we visited Garway, but she was so eager for us to get on our way that she marched us all back outside after just a few minutes.

Then we had to work out how we were all going to get into the car. Dad sat himself in the driver's seat and began checking his road atlas in a 'doesn't affect me' sort of way. Mum began to organise the passengers:

Aunty Amy climbed into the back seat and placed Mark on her knee;

Ann climbed into the back seat next to Aunty Amy;

I climbed into the back seat next to Ann;

Mum put the passenger seat down and climbed into the front seat;

Billy climbed on to Mum's knee;

Mum shut the door.

Then, without looking up from his road atlas, Dad pointed out that if a policeman saw Mum with a child on her knee in the front seat, he would pull us over. He said this firmly but quietly; he was a sea of tranquillity.

'What? Why didn't you say so before?' Mum blasted off.

'You never said you were planning to have him on your knee in the front seat,' Dad said, matter-of-factly.

'What did you think I was meaning, then?'

'I thought you meant that you would sit in the back seat with Amy and then Ann or David would sit in the front seat.'

I wanted to say 'that's a good idea', but I decided against it. Mum looked over her shoulder at the four of us sitting on the back seat. A deep frown on her forehead gave some clue to the intensity of her thought process as she searched for a way out of this. No one spoke. Dad carried on studying his road atlas.

Then, Aunty Amy broke the silence. 'She'll not fit in the back with me, Eric,' she said.

'Oh, I thought you were both slimmer than that,' he laughed.

'That doesn't help, you silly old fool,' Mum admonished.

'I'm not old,' Dad replied, still laughing into his road atlas.

Mum looked at us with grim determination on her face. 'Right,' she announced. 'Billy can lie on the parcel shelf at the back.'

'What!' Dad said in disbelief. But, Mum began to reorganise the passengers anyway:

She opened the door;

Billy climbed out;

Mum climbed out and pulled the passenger seat forward;

I climbed out;

Ann climbed out;

Aunty Amy and Mark stayed where they were.

Then–

Billy climbed in and on to the parcel shelf;

Ann climbed in next to Aunty Amy;

I climbed in next to Ann;

Mum pushed the passenger seat back and climbed into the front seat;

She shut the door.

'Right, that's that sorted,' she concluded.

'Are we ready to go now?' Dad put away his road atlas and turned the ignition key. The little engine started. Then, just as we were about to pull away, there was a loud 'crack' from the back of the car.

'Oo-er,' cried Aunty Amy, craning around. 'Billy's opened the back window!'

Another unique feature of the Hillman Imp was a rear window that was hinged at the top and could be opened from the inside. Billy had found the handle and turned it.

'If he does that while I'm driving,' said Dad, 'he'll roll out the back and end up in the middle of the berloody road.'

Mum turned around, glaring at Billy who by now was wearing a grin that could only be described as, well, impish. She then ordered the two of us to swap places.

'What about me wrist?' I objected.

'Lie on your left side,' she instructed.

Neither Billy nor I wished to move from our respective positions but we were getting the hang of reading the signs. We realised that Mum had found a solution to her problem and now that her mind was made up, any resistance would be futile. So, once more we went through the rigmarole of emptying and refilling the car, but this time ending with me lying on the parcel shelf. Mum regained the front seat and with an air of triumphant finality, shut the passenger door.

And that's how we set out for Loggerheads, with me lying on the parcel shelf with my head propped up on my elbow. From this position I could see over Ann's head, between Mum and Dad and out through the windscreen to the road ahead. I could also look out of the back window and I had an excellent view of the great steel arch of Runcorn Bridge, which carried us over the River Mersey.

For some reason, once we had left Grandma's, Mum ceased giving Dad advice on how to drive; but he seemed to cope quite well without it. Between Chester and Mold, we stopped for Mum to find a public toilet; she had forgotten to go before we left home. By the time we arrived at Loggerheads we had been travelling for over an hour. It was getting to be quite uncomfortable lying on the parcel shelf. My muscles were aching, I was extremely hot and I was beginning to feel a bit sick.

We turned around at the Loggerheads Inn and then pulled over at the roadside. When Dad switched off the engine, I told him I could hear a hissing sound coming from somewhere beneath me. 'It's the cooling system,' he said. 'Doug told me Imps sometimes have problems with the cooling system, with it being a rear-mounted engine. I should have checked the radiator level before I left. I'll sort it out before we return. It'll be alright.'

We all piled out. I was the last one out and I was grateful to be able to stretch my muscles and breathe in the fresh air. That sometimes-sweet sometimes-sour smell of cow muck told you straight away that you were out in the countryside; it smelled just like the cattle tent at Woolton Show. I inhaled deeply through my nose and immediately felt invigorated. Maybe an hour on the parcel shelf was a price worth paying after all. I suggested that the first thing we could do was to take a walk alongside the River Alyn. This was met with approval from all, as we would be sheltered from the fresh breeze.

The 'Leete' walk was just as I remembered it from my school field trip. This little waterway had been constructed to divert water from the river to power lead mining machinery. As we walked along the bank I scoured the surface of the river for signs of movement. Then, to my great delight, I spied what I had been searching for.

'Dipper!' I announced and pointed at a pied torpedo as it skimmed along inches above the surface of the flowing river. The brilliant white breast of this fat and lively bird made it easy to identify, but its rapid flight up and down stream meant you had to be quick to catch a glimpse. On this occasion, due to my alertness, everyone saw it. I told them how unusual this bird was and described how it 'flew' underwater in order to catch its prey. The adults seemed suitably impressed with my knowledge of ornithology.

After half an hour we halted and headed back to the tea-house and gardens. Ann and I walked to the car with Dad to get the folding chairs and the shopping bag, but when Dad opened the boot, we were greeted by the smell of sour milk. Upon further inspection we found that one of the thermos flasks had been leaking and milk had seeped out into the boot. The car had been parked in direct sunlight and the spilt milk had quickly soured. Dad used his handkerchief to mop up as much as he could. 'No use crying over spilt milk,' he joked.

We returned and set up the chairs for the adults. While Mum poured out drinks from the flasks, Dad took us four children into the teahouse and bought ice creams for us. Then we all sat out on the lawn enjoying the sunshine. Everyone agreed that this was a great choice for a day out.

I suggested going for a walk up the footpath that led to the top of the cliff. Mum and Aunty Amy opted to stay and play with Mark on the lawn. So, I led Dad, Ann and Billy up the cliff footpath. At the top there was a metal bench, fixed into the limestone, from which we could look out across the

Clwydian Hills; it was like the picture of the Promised Land in the Children's Illustrated Bible.

The four of us sat on the bench to catch our breath, enjoy the cool breeze and take in the view. I pointed out Moel Famau and Moel Fenlli ahead of us and Colomendy Field Studies Centre to our left. Below us we could make out the Loggerheads Inn, nestling beside the road to Ruthin. 'Logg-er-heads,' said Billy. 'That's a funny name.'

'I've heard of the term "at loggerheads",' said Ann, 'but what does it mean?'

'It's a kind of sea turtle,' I immediately responded.

'Well, that may well be,' said Dad. 'But, the way Ann is using the word it means "to be in disagreement". The story goes that back in the 1700s there was a boundary dispute between two landowners and it was the landlord of the Loggerheads Inn who called a meeting to try to sort it out. That's where the phrase "at loggerheads" comes from.' Although he could not say whether or not the argument was settled, he told us that the sign at the Loggerheads Inn now showed two people in disagreement.

'Are you and me mum ever at loggerheads?' Ann asked him.

'Hardly ever, really,' he replied. 'I suppose that's because as well as being man and wife, we have always been good friends. I've always thought that life is too short to spend it arguing. Besides, most things can be sorted out with a bit of compromise.'

'What does compromise mean?' I said.

'Compromise? Well, it's when you don't get exactly what you want because you consider the needs or wishes of others. Or, sometimes things don't work out how you expected them to, so then you have to change your expectations. I guess it's just one of those lessons of life. You learn that sometimes you have to compromise.'

'What about coming here?' Ann asked him. 'You weren't in agreement about that at the beginning, were you?'

'Ha! The compromise there was that your mum would be in charge of organising the passengers!'

'Do you think we could compromise for me to sit in the front on the way home?' I enquired.

'You had better ask your mum about that,' he laughed. 'Speaking of which, we'd better get going or she'll be wondering where we are.'

We set off back down the steep footpath. On our way back to the tea gardens we walked past the inn to take a look at the sign. 'If there are just two people arguing,' I mused, 'why does the sign say "We Three Loggerheads"?'

We stared at the sign trying to solve the puzzle. 'Maybe the third loggerhead is the person looking at the painting,' suggested Ann.

I said that that didn't make sense. She insisted it did.

'Whatever it means, let's not argue about it. Otherwise we'll be at loggerheads at Loggerheads,' laughed Dad.

Ann and I looked at each other, groaned and rolled our eyes.

We returned to the tea gardens, where Mum, Aunty Amy and Mark were still sitting. Mum announced that she and Aunty Amy would change places for the journey back. She would sit in the back with Mark on her knee so that Aunty Amy could enjoy a bit more legroom in the front seat. When I asked her if I could have a turn in the front seat she insisted that I didn't need to, whereas Aunty Amy did. I asked if someone else could go on the parcel shelf so that I could at least sit down. She argued that Ann was too big and that Billy couldn't be trusted not to open the window, and my protests that this was unfair were dismissed out of hand; so much for compromise, I thought to myself.

We folded up the chairs and returned to the car. I climbed on to the parcel shelf, and Ann and Billy then got in, followed by Mum. Aunty Amy handed Mark to Mum before putting the front seat down, climbing in and closing the door. It was then that we all noticed the sickly smell of sour milk.

'That reminds me,' said Dad. He got out of the car, retrieved the two thermos flasks from under the front bonnet and went down to the river to fill them. When he returned he opened the back of the car and began topping up the radiator.

'You alright, David,' said Mum.

I knew that it was meant to be more of a statement rather than a question, but I replied anyway. 'No,' I said. 'I can't see the road any more. All I can see is the back of your head.'

'Well. I need to sit here because there isn't enough legroom for me behind the driver's seat. Why don't you lie the other way around?'

'Because I can't lay on me right arm,' I reminded her.

She took a deep breath. 'I'm not going to have everybody getting out of the car again while I change places, so you'll just have to put up with it. Besides, coming here was your idea in the first place,' she added.

I thought better of reminding her that it was not my idea to set a new Guinness record for the number of people in a Hillman Imp; I could read the signs. Dad got back in and we set off for home.

As we travelled, I noticed that without being able to see the road I could not anticipate the movement of the car and my insides seem to move every time we went around a bend or changed gear. After a while I was beginning to feel ill. I complained about not being able to see the road, about the smell of sour milk, about my discomfort in lying down, about the heat being generated by the engine beneath me. Mum simply said that there was nothing we could do about those things.

'Can't we compromise?' I suggested. Dad laughed. Mum told me to stop complaining. I was beginning to have serious doubts about whether a day in the countryside was worth this amount of suffering.

I tried to peer around her head but her new perm presented quite a barrier. I tried to push it out of the way but she went mad when I touched it. She said that perm was going to have to last her another eight weeks and that I was not to spoil it.

I began to notice another smell mixing with the sour milk – it was the perm. I didn't know what cocktail of chemicals was used to create a beautiful perm but from where I was lying there was nothing beautiful about the odour it was now giving off. It was right in front of my face. I complained again. Mum said we would be home in twenty minutes.

Ten minutes from home, two things happened almost simultaneously. The first was that I discovered I suffered from car sickness. The second was that I gave Mum a perm the likes of which she had never had before.

'Last time Dave travels on the parcel shelf, then,' said Dad. It wasn't a question.

Chapter Seventeen

SPILT MILK

The nausea of car sickness only served to increase my appreciation of horse-drawn transport. I could not wait to get back on the milk round and it had been agreed that I would do the top round today. Dad and Uncle George would take Rupert 'under the bridge' on the bottom round and then Dad and I would take Peggy 'over the bridge' on the top round.

Mum had decided that as she was going to church to do the brasses, she would walk all three of us down to the dairy, in time for me to meet up with Dad. There was no mention as to what Ann and Billy would do at the dairy. Their presence generated a certain resentment on my part as I did not want them intruding on my time working with Dad. But, I told myself that although this situation was not ideal, I would just have to compromise.

When we arrived at the dairy, Nana and Granddad were in the kitchen. We all marched in to greet them and Mum began to explain where she was going and when she would be calling back. In the middle of this explanation I heard the clip-clop of Rupert's hooves coming up Duke Street; they were returning from the bottom round.

'Yeah!' I exclaimed and bolted down the kitchen steps. Billy was hot on my heels. Before I had reached the doorway of the dairy on to Duke Street, Mum was shouting for us to stop.

'Don't run! David! Stop! Billy! Stop!'

Why stop? Didn't she realise that I knew exactly what I was doing? I had been working with Dad for nearly five weeks now. I knew about the milk van and I knew about horses. I knew what I was doing. I wasn't a child any more.

'Billy! Stop!'

Then I realised that it wasn't me that she was concerned about – it was Billy. He hadn't been working with Dad for weeks as I had. He didn't know what I knew. But he was following me; that was why Mum wanted me to stop. This was exactly what I feared when it had been announced that we were all going down to the dairy. When I was working with Dad, I was treated like an adult and that made me feel so good. But when I was with my family, I was treated like a child. How I resented that – I was too old now for that sort of stuff.

Mum would go mental if I did not stop. She might even stop me working with Dad if something happened to Billy. I stopped. I had just stepped out of the dairy on to Duke Street and I could see the van approaching the stable yard gates, and I stopped. Berloody Billy getting in the berloody way, as always.

At that moment I hated him more than I had ever hated him before.

But Billy did not stop. He ran past me towards the oncoming van. Mum came dashing out of the dairy and caught up with me. Realising that I had stopped but that Billy was still in full flight, she shouted after him, the panic starting to rise in her voice.

'Billy! Stop! Billy! Stop!'

But Billy did not take a blind bit of notice. I feared the consequences of defying Mum but clearly he didn't. I knew that I would never have gotten away with that, but he was the youngest; he was her favourite. Surely, on this occasion he would be bound to get into real trouble for such blatant defiance. If it affected me working with Dad, then I wished it on him.

Uncle George was driving Rupert and he had the horse going at a slow trot as he turned him into the stable yard. Dad was in the right-hand doorway of the van and he could see Billy running towards him.

'Eric! Eric! Watch Billy! Stop him!' Mum shouted.

But Billy did not stop. What happened next seemed to unfold before me in slow motion.

As the van swung around and Rupert passed through the gates to the stable yard, he slowed from a trot to a quick walk. Billy made for Dad, standing in the doorway, and tried to mount the moving van. He grabbed either side of the doorway with his hands and managed to get his right foot onto the step. But he wasn't strong enough to pull himself up. As his left foot lifted from the ground he began to fall backwards. Billy's body pivoted around his right foot and he tried to gain the step with his left foot. He missed the step and his left leg swung under it, into the void beneath the van. This added momentum broke his handholds and he fell backwards on to the ground. Dad tried to grab him but he was inches away.

The van continued to roll forward. Billy's left leg lay in the path of the rear wheel. I could see it coming – why couldn't he? Why didn't he pull his leg away? It seemed to me that he had plenty of time to do it.

Dad could see it coming too, but as the doorway of the van drew opposite the stable yard gatepost, he was unable to get out. He was helpless to do anything except shout to Uncle George to stop. But it takes a second for an instruction to be passed before a horse responds and in that second the rear wheel ran over Billy's leg. He screamed.

'Me baby! Me baby!' Mum screamed in response and ran past me.

Uncle George was unable to see what was going on under and to the rear of the van. At Dad's call he had pulled heavily on the reins to stop the horse. When you pull on the reins that heavily a horse won't just stop, it will instead begin to walk backwards, and that was just what Rupert began to do – he danced two steps back. Dad could see that the wheel was rolling back towards Billy.

'No! Go forward, George!' he shouted as he struggled to find enough space to squeeze out and jump down from the doorway. In response, Uncle George flicked the reins to send Rupert forward. The outcome of this exchange and the second's delay in these instructions being passed from Dad to Uncle George and then on to the horse resulted in the wheel passing backwards over Billy's leg and then to everyone's horror, before Dad could intervene, it passed over it a third time as the horse danced forward again. With each pass of the wheel Billy screamed louder. Why didn't he pull his ber-loody leg from under the van? Why did he just lay there?

'Berloody 'ell!' came the strangulated shout from Dad as he jumped down.

'Me baby! Me baby!' Mum screamed again as she ran towards him.

Dad was the first to reach Billy. He scooped him up. Then Mum took the screaming child from him and ran back towards the dairy. I stood there frozen. As she passed me she was crying aloud and I could see the tears running down her face. Billy was in her arms and he was still screaming. Nana and Granddad had come to the dairy door just in time to witness what had taken place.

'Get an ambulance! Get an ambulance!' Mum shouted as she pushed past them and ran back into the dairy. I could hear Billy's cries receding as Mum went into the house. As I looked back down Duke Street I could see that the commotion had brought people to their doors. Dad followed the van into the yard. I heard him shout to Uncle George that the wheel had gone over Billy's leg. I went into the covered yard of the dairy and then Dad appeared running in from the jigger entrance.

Where is he?' Dad demanded.

'Alice has him inside,' said Granddad. 'She wants an ambulance.'

'I don't think so,' said Dad as he strode up the kitchen steps. 'It's a pneumatic tyre. It's probably just pinched him.' With that he disappeared into the house. Nana and Granddad followed him. 'You're best to wait here,' Granddad said to me as they went inside.

I waited in the covered yard, feeling numbed by what I had witnessed. Ann came out of the house. She had missed it all.

She asked me what was going on, why Billy was crying, why Granddad had sent her outside. I described to her what had taken place.

The crying from inside seemed to have stopped. Uncle George appeared from the jigger entrance and walked into the house in silence. After a few minutes he and Dad came back out. Uncle George didn't say anything; he just walked back through to the stable yard. Dad came over to us. He told us not to worry, that Billy would be okay. He said that the tyre had pinched Billy's leg but it did not look like anything was broken.

'I've had the van run over my foot on more than one occasion,' he said. 'It's not the most comfortable of experiences, but it didn't do any damage.'

'What about all the screaming?' I said.

'That was probably just shock,' he replied. 'He was probably screaming in fear as much as in pain. I think it was a shock to us all, especially Alice. She's inside, having a cup of sweet tea.'

'What's going to happen now?' Ann said.

'Alice is going to take Billy to Garston Hospital to make sure he's okay. Nana and Granddad still have the old baby buggy, so she will put him in that to save having to carry him.'

I hesitated. 'What's happening with the top round?' I didn't like to ask but I still wanted to know.

'Erm, let me have a word with George first and then I'll tell you,' Dad replied. With that he left us and walked through to the stable yard.

Granddad came out of the house and asked us if we were okay. He said we could go inside now if we wanted to. He went into the cold room and emerged carrying the old baby buggy. I hadn't seen that for years. I could remember being pushed to and from the dairy in that buggy when I was very young. Billy had been the last of us to use it. Granddad unfolded it. We left him wiping it down and went in to see how Billy was.

Mum was sitting in an armchair with Billy on her lap. His face was buried in her bosom and he was still whimpering. His left leg was held out straight, resting on the arm of the chair. Mum was sipping a cup of tea while Nana busied herself changing a cold flannel, which covered Billy's knee and shin.

I was half expecting a blast from Mum for my part in the incident. Instead, to my surprise, she apologised if she had frightened me with her screaming. I didn't know how to respond. I had never received an apology from Mum before. She seemed to be in full control of herself now and even seemed a little embarrassed about her earlier outburst of emotion. When Granddad came in to say that the buggy was ready, she thanked them both politely for their help and carried Billy outside. We all followed her. Dad was in the covered yard, checking the buggy. He lifted it outside on to the pavement and Mum put Billy into it. We all watched as she set off down Duke Street, pushing Billy in the buggy.

My grandparents and Ann went back into the house but Dad took me to one side. He told me that he would do the top round with Uncle George. He said that Uncle George was upset about what had happened to Billy and then he said something about when you fall off a bike, the best thing to do is get back on it straight away. I wasn't sure what bikes had to do with the situation but I had no inclination to argue my case. I had been expecting a whole lot worse than missing one top round and besides, it didn't seem that important now. Not after what had happened to Billy.

I watched from the dairy doorway as Uncle George drove Peggy up Duke Street in the milk float. Dad waved to me as they disappeared around the corner into Wellington Street. I sat on the step for a while. I didn't feel like going back into the house, I wanted to be on my own.

I dragged my feet down to the stable yard. The van was standing there, alone, as if it was in disgrace. I crouched down and looked underneath. There was plenty of clearance. There was no way you could be crushed under there. I examined the rear wheel that had gone over Billy. I kicked it to test its hardness. My foot bounced back off its inflated walls. I sat myself on the step of the van and reran the event in my mind.

When Billy had first followed me out of the dairy I had been angry with him. It was that usual feeling of injustice that I was not allowed to do what my two-years-older sister was allowed to do, plus I was not allowed to do the things that my three-years-younger brother was not allowed to do. I blamed Mum for this injustice. I was angry at her for always stopping me doing what I wanted to do. In fact, if she hadn't stopped me from running, I would have got to the van first and I would have stopped Billy trying to climb on, or I would have been there to pull him away before the wheel could run over his leg.

Then I remembered her crying out 'Me baby!' and all my blame disappeared. There had been so much fear in that cry. It rang out in my head – Me baby! – and made the tears well in my eyes. It struck me that she must have thought that Billy was going to be killed, right there in front of her. Me baby! That must have been terrible for her. If I had not stopped running I could have been there and changed things. I could have saved Billy. Me baby! That's what older brothers are supposed to do, dammit.

I wandered around the van and reran the scene again and again in my head, but each time I would change something I had done and then imagine a different outcome. What would have happened if I had done this? What if I had done that? I shuffled into the shippon and sat on the hay bales and reran the scene. I skulked into the old stable and climbed into the hayloft and reran the scene. I mooched over to Danny's stable and gazed in to the empty space and reran the scene.

I must have been daydreaming like this for quite some time when I heard the buggy rattle across the cobbles at the entrance to the yard. Mum and Billy were back from the hospital. They were both smiling – a million miles from the scene of a couple of hours ago. Billy was riding in the buggy with a bandage around his leg and he was sucking on an ice lolly. I felt a huge wave of relief wash over me; it was so good to see them both happy and well again. I followed them into the covered yard.

'Is he okay?' I asked Mum.

'He's fine,' she smiled. 'And he has something for you.'

Billy held out his hand with something pressed under his thumb. I took it from him and looked at it. I gasped. It was an 'On Safari' card. But not just any 'On Safari' card; it was number eight – the leopard.

'You won't believe this,' she said. 'But, when we came out of the hospital I asked him if he wanted an ice cream from Bob's. He said no, let's buy a Fab and see if we can get Dave his last card. That is the one you want, isn't it?'

'Yeah. Yeah. That's it. That's the one.' I looked at Billy. 'Thank you,' I managed. He just smiled back at me and continued to suck on his ice lolly.

At that moment I loved him more than I had ever loved him before.

Just then, Nana and Granddad came out of the house. Mum described to them what had happened at the hospital. Billy had had an X-ray, but there were no bones broken. They invited her in for another cup of tea; a bit less sugar this time. She carried Billy inside.

I looked again at the picture card. As I stood there I heard the distant sound of horse's hooves; the milk float was returning. I placed the card safely in my pocket and walked back to the stable yard. I stood in the lean-to as Uncle George drove Peggy into the yard and pulled her up just behind the parked van. Dad jumped down from the back of the float and chocked one of the big wooden wheels. He greeted me as he walked forward to begin unhitching the horse.

Uncle George gave up the reins to Dad and bent to pick up three bottles of sterrie to take in for Aunty Mary. He had huge hands and could carry four bottles of sterrie in each, the narrow necks held firm between each of his fingers. As he stepped down from the back of the float he seemed to lose his balance. He managed to hold on with his left hand, but as he swung around, his right hand, carrying the three bottles, slammed into the body of the float. This jar was enough to free the bottles from his grip and they fell onto the cobbled floor. There wasn't the crashing sound of breaking glass, but more of a popping sploosh as all three bottles burst on the ground. An implosion of white covered the cobbles.

'Aww, berloody 'ell,' muttered Uncle George.

'Ayup!' shouted Dad. 'You alright, George?' He ran to the back of the float. I ran after him.

Uncle George sat himself on the rear step. 'A fine owjadoo – just a bit dizzy, is all,' he said. 'Must have stood up too quick.'

I looked at him. For the first time that I could recall, Uncle George looked old. In my mind he had always been a tough, rough-hewn sort who worked like, well, like a horse. But now he looked pale and frail. His clogs looked massive on him, as if they were too heavy for him to lift.

We waited in silence while he regained himself and then he stood up slowly. Dad told him to go on in. 'Dave and I'll see to the horse and I'll pop in with a couple of sterrie when we're finished.'

I expected Uncle George to object, to decline this offer, but to my surprise he nodded his head in agreement. 'Alright,' he said. 'I'll see you later.' He gave the two of us a half-hearted smile and then we watched him amble through the lean-to and into the jigger, his clogs scraping on the ground as he went.

Dad unloaded the remaining milk from the float and then asked me to help him unhitch Peggy. The horse stood still, waiting patiently while the two of us rolled the float away from her and then backed it into the lean-to, where we rested it on its shafts. Dad closed the gates to the yard. He took a plastic bucket from Danny's stable and carefully picked up the pieces of broken milk bottle, placing them into the bucket. He then tipped the broken glass into a metal dustbin in the lean-to and took the bucket into the water shed. He filled the bucket a couple of times and used it to swill the spilt milk down the grid in the corner of the yard.

While he was busy tidying up, Peggy waited patiently. Once done, he led her into the shippon; I followed. He went about this work with only an occasional word to me. Was he angry with me? Was he thinking about Uncle George? Then I remembered that Uncle George had been upset about Billy and I hurriedly told Dad that Billy was back from the hospital and that nothing was broken.

'That's good news,' he nodded as he began to untack Peggy. 'I'll tell George when I take his milk through.'

I waited until he had finished untacking and had Peggy in her stall. 'Does this mean it's all over?' I ventured.

He looked at me, thoughtfully. 'Is what all over?'

'You know. Me working with you. Because of what happened to Billy.'

'Oh, that. No, no. That wasn't your fault. That was just an accident,' he said. And then, 'but there is something I need to talk to you about. Come and sit down over here.' He nodded towards the hay bales. We both walked over and sat down next to each other.

'You know that your granddad can't do much work around the dairy now, don't you?'

'Yeah,' I replied, as my expectations began to rise.

'Well, Uncle George is getting old also – too old to carry on working. He's decided it's time for him to retire ...'

My expectations soared. I knew what was coming next. Dad was going to ask me about taking over from Uncle George and working with him on the rounds; like D'Artagnan joining the Three Musketeers! I had already given this some thought, how we could work it once my wrist had healed. On weekdays, before I went to school, I could get up early and do the bottom round with him and Rupert. He would then be able to do the top round on his own with Peggy and drop me off at school on the way. I would be able to go to the dairy straight after school and help him with the horses before tea. On Saturday mornings we could do the two rounds together and then on Saturday afternoons we could do the runs to the smithy and to the docks as and when we needed. The two of us could do it together. It was perfect: 'A. Joy & Sons' – we wouldn't even have to change the sign!

'... and so we're going to have to sell the dairy.'

'What?' I had heard what he had said. The question was a reflex. Something your brain does to give it time to understand what has been said and to grasp the implications. 'What?' I repeated.

'We're going to sell the dairy,' Dad repeated. 'It's all been sorted out. I'm going to ...'

I didn't hear anything else he said; my brain was still catching up. Thoughts came to me in a kaleidoscope: the Joy family grave; the lineage of farmers; Garston Park; Dale Farm; Wellington Dairy; the milk rounds; the sawdust run; Bernard Vanstone and the smithy; Danny, Rupert and Peggy; the stable yard; the shippon; the Duke Street Kids; Uncle George, Granddad and Dad. Dad – working with me dad. I couldn't breathe properly. I began to gulp air, but I couldn't breathe out. It was like being winded and having asthma all at the same time. I began to feel dizzy. I heard Dad ask me if I was alright but I couldn't answer him. He grabbed my shoulders and asked me again. He shook me and then slapped me on the back. When I did exhale it came out as an enormous sob.

'I wanted to be the next 'A. Joy',' I cried. The dam burst; the tears flowed and my body shook as I began to sob uncontrollably.

Dad looked at me, shocked, before realisation dawned. 'Oh Dave,' he said. 'I ... I didn't know.' He put his arm around my shoulders. 'I'm so sorry. I didn't know you felt like that.'

We sat like that while I cried my heart out. We sat like that while my tears flowed and swilled away my dreams; like spilt milk, swilled down the grid in the corner of the yard. We sat like that until my reservoir of tears was empty and until the sobs had so exhausted my lungs that my chest ached and I could sob no more. 'Let it all out, son,' whispered Dad as he waited patiently for me to recover. Eventually, I stopped sobbing and began to catch my breath. 'What about you?' I managed. 'What will you do?'

'That's what I was just telling you. Your Uncle Ed has managed to get me a job on the docks. I'm going to be a 'Checker' with Irish Sea Ferries.'

He announced this with some degree of pride. I wiped my eyes and asked him what that meant and he told me he would be checking all of the containers that would be coming in and going out of the docks, to make sure they all arrived and departed when they should and to make sure none went missing.

As he spoke I started to put the pieces of the puzzle together: the meetings with Uncle Ed; the hushed conversations in the front room; Dad 'on business' in the docks office, talking about a 'cheque' that was actually a 'Checker'; learning to drive and buying a car. It all began to make sense.

He told me he would be starting the week after next; the same week that I started my new school. 'So it's going to be a big change for all of us,' he said. 'Uncle George will be retiring, I'll have a new job and you'll be going to a new school. Big changes. And big challenges – for all of us.'

'The times, they are a-changin',' I mused.

'Aye, that's exactly right,' he laughed.

I thought about all of the changes that were taking place, trying to work out all of the implications. 'What about all of our customers?' I said. 'Who'll deliver the milk if we don't do it?'

'We've sold the top round and the bottom round as two separate businesses. They've both been bought by milkmen who do the adjacent rounds.'

'But what about Wellington Dairy?' I said. 'What about the buildings and the yard?'

'Your nana and granddad will carry on living at 37 Wellington Street, but we are selling the stable yard to a builder. He's going to use it as a builder's yard.'

'The bloke in the green boiler suit?' Another piece in the puzzle.

'Yes, that's him. Mr Long. He's a local builder and he wants to move to bigger premises. He'll convert the shippon and the other buildings to give him a good-sized depot.'

A sudden fear struck me. 'What about the horses? You're not going to have them put down are you?'

'Hell, no. They're not old, like Danny was. They're still good working horses, both of them. We've managed to find a local buyer for Rupert.'

'The man in the donkey jacket?'

Dad laughed. 'Aye, that's right. Tommy Atkins. I've known him for many years. He's got some fields out at Halewood. Rupert will like it there.' I asked about Peggy and he told me that she would be sent to auction. 'Don't worry,' he said. 'We won't sell her to just anyone. We'll make sure she gets a good home.'

I pondered on this new information. 'When was all of this decided?'

'Well, we started thinking about it last year, after your Uncle George's seventy-fifth birthday.'

My head began to clear. A big drip appeared at the end of my nose and I sniffed it up. Dad passed me his handkerchief. It was filthy. I blew hard. 'So, it's all settled then; all sorted out?' I said.

'Yes, it's all done and dusted, so dry your eyes. Anyroad, you know what they say, don't you?'

'What?'

'There's no point in crying ...'

'... over spilt milk,' I completed.

We both managed a laugh – just a small one.

Chapter Eighteen

THE LAST OF THE MOHICANS

I tried to make that final week at the dairy last forever. I went on every round. And, in a display of willingness and willpower, I even rode the muck cart. Dad had to empty the midden and we took it all down to the allotments next to the 'botullwerks'. The muck at the bottom of the midden had almost turned into soil. There were a number of other things to do to prepare for the sale of the business.

On the Monday I had a special duty to carry out. We had a letter printed to give to all of our customers. On both rounds it was my job to post a copy through every customer's letterbox. I could manage this despite the splint on my right wrist. The letter told the customer that after one hundred years of providing fresh milk to the doorstep, A. Joy & Sons were retiring. It said that our last delivery would be on Saturday and told them who would be delivering their milk on the following Monday. We thanked them for their long and loyal custom and wished them well.

Although Peggy had recently had her hind feet shod, we took her up to the smithy to have all her shoes checked.

After Bernard had looked at her, Dad decided to have her two fore shoes replaced; he wanted her to be in the best possible condition when she went to auction. As I watched the shoeing take place, Old Mr Vanstone came over to talk to me. I told him that I had so wanted to replace Uncle George but everyone had said that I was too young.

'Nay, lad,' he shook his head. 'There's not much call for horsemen nowadays. They're a dying breed. You go and get yersel' a good education and once you've got some qualifications, then yer can decide what it is yer want to do for a living.'

'I'd still like to work with horses,' I said.

'Aye. Well, maybe. Maybe. We'll just have to wait and see. Yer'll have plenty of time to make yer mind up.'

After Dad had paid up, Old Mr Vanstone and Bernard came to the smithy gates to see us off. Bernard came over to me and shook my hand. 'Well, meladdo,' he grinned. 'I guess we'll not be seeing thee around here no more. Well, it's been nice knowing yer. You just make sure yer take care of this old dad of yours, won't yer?'

'I'm not old,' objected Dad. We all laughed. Then we said our farewells and they waved us off for the last time. It was like that whatever we did: the last time. Although I was enjoying everything we were doing, it was all tinged with sadness.

On the way back to the dairy we passed the Duke Street Kids, sitting on Falco's doorstep. While Dad unhitched Peggy, I walked back down the street to talk to them. I told them about us selling the dairy and Dad getting a job down on the docks. We talked about having one last play in the shippon. I said we could do it once I'd finished working with Dad. I told them I'd see them later.

A horsebox came for Peggy on the Friday of that final week. To get her ready for auction, we had groomed her coat until it shone. I decided not to accompany Dad and Uncle George to the auction as I thought it would have been too sad to see her go like that. But, when they returned they told me that a taxi company in Blackpool had bought her, so she would be pulling holidaymakers along the Golden Mile in a landau. Wow! Imagine that. It would be like being on holiday all the time. She would like that. I was just a tiny bit jealous.

On the Saturday, the last day of business, Rupert did both rounds. It was a sad but special day for the family. On the bottom round Ann, Billy and Granddad all came along as well. Never before had we had so many passengers, but the van was easily big enough for us all and Rupert was more than a match for the task. When we reached the top of Windfield Road, something strange began to happen. Normally the road would be deserted at this time of the morning; it was only occasionally that someone needed to come to the door to sort something out. But this morning it seemed that all of our customers had come to their doors.

They had been waiting for the sound of the horse's hooves and then had made a point of coming out to say 'thank you' to Dad and Uncle George. Some of them had small gifts; nothing expensive, things like home-made cake, biscuits or wine. Some of them came out to pat Rupert and feed him carrots. Others just stood on their doorsteps and waved or even clapped as we went past. A number of older people came over to talk to Granddad; they knew him from the days when he did the rounds. It happened all the way around the estate.

I could hear Dad calling 'thank you very much' as he moved from one house to the next. When he came back to the van to fill up his crate he passed the gifts in to us and we placed them carefully at the front of the van. He was smiling from sticky-out-ear to sticky-out-ear. Even Uncle George had a smile on his face. By the time we had finished the round we had a pile of gifts. 'Berloody 'ell,' chuckled Dad. 'What the hell are we going to do with all this stuff?'

We travelled back to the dairy feeling like kings – rich with goodwill. We were running late so it was decided that we would do the top round in the van also, in order to save time. Of course, this also meant that we could all go on the top round as well. Dad and Uncle George unloaded the empties from the bottom round and stacked them in the stable yard. Then they transferred the top-round milk from the walk-in refrigerator into the back of the van and we were ready to go.

Once we started delivering in the first street, exactly the same thing happened as before. Everyone came out to see us. Someone even came out and tied a strip of bunting along the side of the van. We felt like we were in a parade. 'Hell's bells,' laughed Dad. 'It's like ruddy VE Day!'

When we finally arrived back at the dairy, Uncle George sorted out which of the gifts he would take for Aunty Mary and we three kids carried the rest of the stuff into the house while the adults saw to Rupert. Nana couldn't believe it when we marched in, overloaded with gifts. We sat down in the living room, exhausted yet euphoric. It was a sad day, but the customers had made it an extra special day.

On the Sunday, we didn't go to church in the morning as it had been arranged for Tommy Atkins to come and collect Rupert. Because he was going to be local, Dad decided that we would follow him out to Halewood, to see him in his new home. Granddad, Ann, Billy and I all travelled in the Imp with Dad. When we arrived at Halewood we watched as Rupert was unloaded and turned out into one of the fields. He looked very happy in his new home, with so much space.

The Monday was Dad's first day in his new job. Early in the morning he set out on his bike the way he had always done, but this time he took a packed lunch with him. All through the day Mum kept on saying, 'I wonder how your dad's getting on in his new job.'

Later in the morning Mum took me down to the hospital to have my splint removed. As we walked past the end of James Street, who should come around the corner but Steven Scales. This was the first time I had seen him since the fight. I folded my arms to keep my right hand out of sight. For a moment we made eye contact. I was expecting him to give me one of his smarmy grins, but instead he just dropped his eyes and walked past in silence. To my great satisfaction I realised that there was an absence of butterflies. There was a tension, a readiness for action, but there was no fear. I took a moment to explore this new condition. It felt good.

At the hospital my splint was removed. My right wrist seemed to be a bit thinner than my left. The doctor showed me some simple flexing exercises that would help to strengthen the muscles in my right forearm. I practised these as we walked home. It was as we reached the top of Chapel Road that it struck me – at this time of day you would normally hear the sound of the horse's hooves doing the top round – but no more.

When we arrived home, Ann was in her room reading and Billy was out playing with his friends. I didn't feel like playing out. I spent most of the afternoon in my room, reading back issues of *TV21* or studying my now complete 'On Safari' wallchart. The day dragged. I missed not being able to work with Dad. All I had to look forward to was starting my new school in the morning, but I tried not to think about that too much; it just depressed me even more.

Dad came home at six o'clock and we sat down for tea to hear all about his day. He told us that he already knew many of the people he would be working with, as most came from Garston and some were his milk customers. He said that they all had nicknames that went with their surnames: 'Legga' Lamb, 'Owton' Bale, 'Glassa' Andrews, 'Persil' White, 'Ampton' Court, 'Opalong' Cassidy, 'Sweeney' Todd, 'Desperate' Dunne and 'Theo' Bailey. Dad had not been given a nickname yet, as most of them already knew him as 'Eck'.

He told us that he would be working shifts according to the tide times. We were quite used to him being up at the crack of dawn, but him working late into the night would be a new experience for all of us. He said that most of the time he would be working out of doors on the dockside or in the goodsies, but that there would be some office work as he had to keep records up to date; in that respect it was going to be similar to running the dairy.

He laughed when he told us how surprised the dock manager had been when he was able to work out in his head whether or not a container was going to be able to fit in a ship's cargo hold. 'I used Pythagoras' theorem,' he grinned. 'I knew those night-school classes would come in handy one day!'

The conversation moved on and Mum asked how I wanted to get to school in the morning. I admitted that I hadn't given this any thought whatsoever. I didn't even know where Quarry Bank was located.

'It's on the junction of Rose Lane and Mather Avenue,' said Dad. 'Opposite the fire station. You can get the No. 80 bus along Brodie Avenue or the No. 86 along Mather Avenue.'

There were only four other kids from St Mary's who were going to Quarry Bank: two girls and two lads. I hadn't been in touch with any of them over the summer holidays as I'd been too busy working with Dad. I knew that some of them had older brothers or sisters at the school, so they would probably go in with them. Ann went to St Hilda's but I was the first Joy to go to Quarry Bank.

It struck me then just how inexperienced I was as a traveller. Before we had the car we walked, cycled or drove the horses most places. When we visited Garway, we would catch the No. 66 bus to Woolton, but we always went there with Mum and Dad. I had never been on a bus journey by myself.

Although Mum described where I needed to catch the bus and where I needed to get off, it must have been clear to her that I was out of my depth. 'It's time you learned to stand on your own two feet,' she chided. Nevertheless, it was decided that she would accompany me on my first morning but that I would buy my own ticket so that I would know how to do it in future. I was not looking forward to this at all. To cheer me up Dad asked me if I wanted to accompany him down to the dairy, as he had a number of things to pick up. I readily agreed and we drove down once we had finished tea. On the way down he asked me if I was looking forward to starting school. I told him I wasn't. He said that everyone gets nervous about major changes in their lives: fear of the unknown, he called it. He said he had felt nervous about starting his new job, but once you do start something new you soon get used to it. 'You just have to grin and bear it,' he advised. I couldn't take much comfort from that.

We arrived at the dairy in no time. The journey took only a matter of minutes in the car. Dad wanted to sort himself out a full set of harness. When I asked him what for, he said that one day, when he retired, he would work with horses again. And when that day came, he wanted to be able to use his own harness. 'Besides,' he reasoned, 'I've been maintaining harness all of my life and it's something I really enjoy doing.' I helped him to carry it through from the shippon to the cold room, where it would keep well.

As we went into the stable yard, I noticed that both the van and the float had gone. 'Yes, we managed to sell them,' confirmed Dad. 'There are other bits and pieces that we are selling as well. Your granddad and Uncle George will sort all that out before we hand over the yard at the end of the week. Some of it will just go for scrap.'

The stable yard used to be full of sound: hooves clopping and scraping, horses neighing and snorting, chickens clucking and crowing. But, now it was quiet. It was more than quiet. It was empty, like a ghost town.

Once we had put the harness in the cold room, Dad said there was just one more thing to do. Uncle George was bringing his ladder around and we were going to take the sign down from the dairy wall. He said he wanted to see if it could be salvaged. We walked around to Uncle George's house and as we entered his backyard, I noticed that the cooing of his pigeons had now been added to by the cluck of hens. He had moved his hens out of the shippon and had put them in one of his spare pigeon lofts.

Dad helped Uncle George lift his long ladder down from on top of the pigeon lofts and the two of them then passed it over the back wall before carrying it down the jigger and around to the front of the house.

There it hung, as it had always hung for as long as I could remember. I read it aloud:

Wellington Dairy

A. Joy & Sons

Farmers and Cowkeepers

Est. 1863

'I always thought that one day that would mean me,' I said.

'It does mean you,' said Dad. 'it means all of us. Granddad, Uncle George, me, you and Billy. We are all sons of Anthony Joy.' I hadn't thought of it like that before. That made me feel a bit better. 'But I won't be "A. Joy, Farmer and Cowkeeper", will I?'

'No,' admitted Dad. 'I'll be the last - The Last of the Mohicans,' he smiled. He looked down at me. 'The world has moved on and now it's time for you, Ann and Billy to take a different path. You will have opportunities that were never open to me and I hope you'll make the most of them.'

Dad stood at the bottom of the ladder and Nana and Granddad came out to watch as Uncle George climbed up with a metal crowbar in his hand. He tried gently to prise the sign away from the wall. With a muffled 'pop' it split right across the middle.

'Aw, it's rotten,' announced Uncle George.

He passed down the two pieces to Dad. But as Dad handled them they began to break up in his hands. 'Hell,' he said. 'It must have been ready to drop off. Good job we took it down when we did.'

'Can we fix it?' I asked.

'No, I'm afraid it's had it, son,' he replied. 'Never mind.'

Granddad called us in to the house. He said that he had something to show us. We went in to the back room. The bureau was open and there were papers scattered everywhere. 'I've been going through all of the business' paperwork,' he explained. 'And I've found one or two interesting things. First of all there's this.' From down the side of the bureau he produced a brown paper bag. 'I believe that you're now the stamp collector in the family,' he said as he handed me the bag.

'Yes. Ann gave me her collection,' I said, to emphasise the point.

'Well, as I've been going through the paperwork, I've been putting all the stamps to one side for you. There's plenty in there and many of them are old ones. That should keep you busy for a while.'

I looked in the bag and pulled out a handful of assorted confetti. I could immediately make out a number of stamps: Elizabeth II 3*d* Purples, George VI 2*d* Oranges and even a George V halfpenny Green. 'Wow!' I exclaimed. 'That's brilliant! Thank you! Thank you!' A present from Granddad – just for me. There was something particularly satisfying about that but I knew straight away that I would share my swaps with Billy. I was about to examine my treasures more closely when Granddad caught my attention once more.

'I've also found this,' he announced to the room in general, holding up a few pages of folded notepaper. I could see that they were typewritten and very faded. 'It's the eulogy that was read out at Anthony Joy's funeral. Read it for us, will you, Eck?' He handed the papers to Dad. I sat next to Nana and Uncle George came in and stood by the door. Dad took off his glasses and read the note aloud.

It said that Anthony Joy was a Yorkshireman by birth but had moved to Garston as a young boy. He had been educated in the church day school and had then worked with his father in the dairy in Railway Street. He had become a well-known and highly respected figure. It listed the things he had done: a choirboy at St Michaels and then a church sidesman for thirty years; a member of the Liverpool & District Farmers and Cowkeepers Association; president of the Garston Hotel Bowling Club; and, a member of the Oddfellows Guild who took an active interest in local politics. It also said that he met his wife through the church and that they had been a standing example of a happy Christian marriage.

It described him as a keen businessman, but a firm and honest one, who always expected and who always gave a square deal; a man of strong opinions but who was always ready to listen to others who saw things from a different angle; and, a man who was held in high esteem and admired for his transparent sincerity.

There was no signature to say who had written the eulogy but when Dad had finished reading it, I felt like I now knew Anthony Joy. He was no longer just a name on the family gravestone or on the Wellington Dairy sign. The demise of that sign had been a sad end to a sad day. But after hearing the eulogy, it felt like more than that; it felt like the sad end to a way of life.

Chapter Nineteen

ONE GIANT LEAP ...

That sadness hung over me through the night and was still with me the following morning when I awoke to face my first day at my new school. Just before he went to work, Dad came in to make sure I was awake and to wish me luck. After he left, I lay there for a while, reflecting on the events of the past week. So much seemed to have changed.

Reluctantly, I stirred myself. I washed and then stood in front of the wardrobe mirror as I put on my new school uniform. When I was finished I hardly recognised myself. Someone else, an older-looking Deejay, was staring back at me.

'The times, they are a'changin', ' Bob Dylan had sung.

Mum had arranged for Billy to walk to school with his friends, so that she could take me. We were going to catch the No. 86 bus at Garston cenotaph. That meant walking diagonally across Garston Park. There were dozens of other kids crossing my path, on their way to New Heys.

'Its time for you to take a different path,' me dad had said.

They all seemed to be walking in groups. No one was walking with parents. I immediately felt embarrassed at this, but even more so when I heard girlie voices taunting 'Mummy! Mummy!' At that moment I wished so much that I had transferred to New Heys when I had the chance.

'No use crying over spilt milk,' me dad had said.

We had to queue for the bus and when we got on it was chokka; there was standing room only. Mum stood slightly away from me. I supposed she was trying to alleviate my embarrassment of having to travel accompanied by her.

When we arrived at the end of Mather Avenue, the bus stop was right outside the gates to the school hall. There were members of staff at the gates, directing a bustling stream of kids into the hall. It was at the school gates that I noticed for the first time that I seemed to be the only boy wearing short trousers and no one was wearing a school cap – I removed mine and stuffed it into my blazer pocket. I said a very quick and quiet 'bye' to Mum, took a deep breath and then leaped in to join the throng.

'One giant leap ....' Neil Armstrong had said.

That was it. I was on my own now. I went with the flow of bodies through the doors of the hall. Once inside, there was a sea of uniforms all sitting in rows; row upon row of anonymous faces. I had never before seen so many kids in one place, not even on Garston Park. It was like the Sermon on the Mount in the Children's Illustrated Bible. As I was jostled along I scanned the faces, looking for any of the other four kids from St Mary's. In my mind I had envisaged that I would meet up with at least one of them, but as I searched for a familiar face I realised that the chances of finding one were zero.

'It's time you learnt to stand on your own two feet,' me mum had said.

We were herded into a row near the back of the hall and I sat down between two lads – two strangers. They both seemed to be with someone and were busy talking to them, both with their backs to me. I sat there acutely aware that mine were the only bare legs on the row. But, Mum had said that Uncle Ron had worn short pants up until the sixth form – and I had seen the photograph. Then the awful truth dawned on me – that had been an old photograph and times had changed. All kids nowadays wore long pants to school. All kids, that is, except me. Oh God. The shame grew inside me as I began to realise just how poorly I had been prepared for this experience. I despaired. Mum! How could you do this to me? Uncle Ron may well have worn short pants at this school – but that was berloody fifteen years ago! I felt the cowardy-custard cabbage whites taking off in my stomach.

The excited hubbub cooled as a tall, well-dressed, elderly looking gentleman walked on to the stage at the front of the hall. He introduced himself as Mr Bell, the headmaster of this, the 'Morrison' wing of Quarry Bank Comprehensive School. As well as welcoming us all, he talked about what school life was going to be like.

'Get yersel' a good education,' Old Mr Vanstone had said.

He finished by telling us what was going to happen next: Mr Williams, the Head of Year, would call out names for each of the nine forms. When your name was called you had to go to the front of the hall to join your form teacher, who would then take you all to your new form room.

I surmised that Mr Williams must be a very important person in this school. He stood on the stage with his chin held high, his lips pursed and his cheeks sucked in. He looked like a grown up version of Tubs. Then, he began the long process of booming out every kid's name, starting with Form 11 and working right through to Form 19. As the list was being read out, I listened out for the names of the four kids from St Mary's. I thought that surely they would put at least two of us in the same form so that we would know someone. As unusual names were called out, the lads on either side of me were making fun of them and laughing with their friends. The process went on and on and gradually the hall began to empty. By the time we had got to the end of Form 16, three of the other four St Mary's kids had left the hall. There was only me and Peter Farron left.

'Form 17,' Mr Williams announced. 'Your form teacher will be Mr Pownall.' I could see a tall, thick-set young teacher stand up at the front of the hall. Mr Williams read out the names in alphabetical order. 'Anthony Armstrong,' he began. My stomach churned at the mention of the name 'Anthony'. I thought it was going to be me. He read on and passed the Fs with no mention of Peter Farron. I hoped I would not hear my name so that we could be in the same form. But, when it came to the Js, there it was: 'Anthony Joy,' he announced.

The lads next to me burst out laughing. I didn't move. I decided to wait until the next name was called. 'John Lewis,' announced Mr Williams.

'Ha! Dicky Lewis! Diddee model for der statue,' came the loud whisper next to me, followed by muffled laughter. Despite this, I stood up, shuffled out of my row and walked to the front of the hall. It felt like everyone's eyes were on me – and on my bare legs. I could hear sniggering and then someone sitting in an aisle seat said 'Ha! Dig his legs!' and the sniggering broke into laughter. I suppressed the urge to run away and I joined the growing group in front of Mr Pownall. I was grateful to be able to hide myself in the crowd.

'*Well done, Deejay,'* Tubs had said.

The list continued until Mr Williams called out 'Peter West.' Then he addressed the group. 'Form 17, please follow Mr Pownall to your new form room.'

As we left the hall, some of the kids were already chatting. Obviously, they knew each other. I knew no one in the form. I ended up walking on my own at the back of the group. I felt so very alone. I wanted to be somewhere else – at home, at the dairy, anywhere but here. I could feel the butterflies in full flight in my stomach. It was like being faced with the prospect of a fight. I felt like running away. The tears were trying to push up under my eyes. But there was no way I was going to cry; that would be the ultimate humiliation.

'*You just have to grin and bear it,'* me dad had said.

I followed the group, winding our way around the buildings. As we walked, Mr Pownall turned and announced that we had a room in the new extension. We all followed on, with me at the rear. Eventually we turned into our new form room and everyone crocodiled in through the door. There was a rush for the seats and I was left standing at the front of the class, alone.

They were double desks with two kids sat at each one. Everyone was anxious to sit next to their friends – I didn't have that problem. There was an excited chatter as people sat down and looked to see who their neighbours were.

As I scanned the classroom for an empty chair, some of the chatter turned to laughter as my situation became apparent. I wanted to get out of there.

'There's a spare seat over here,' said Mr Pownall, pointing to an empty chair.

The spare place was next to a girl. She was busy chatting with her neighbours and had her back to me. The laughter rose again as my predicament was seen to worsen. I knew they were all watching me and I felt my face beginning to flush – worse still, I felt my legs beginning to flush too.

As I walked over to the chair, I fought against my embarrassment. I sat myself down and kept my eyes fixed straight ahead, looking at the blackboard on the front wall of the classroom. Then a voice next to me said, 'Hi. I'm Jean.' I turned, and immediately lost myself in the dark brown smiling eyes of the girl from the launderette.

'*Ah, the Lord works in mysterious ways,*' me mum and dad had said.

EPILOGUE

The year after the dairy closed, we spent a summer vacation in Hebden, searching for our family roots. That, for me, marked the beginning of a life-long love affair with the Yorkshire Dales.

Dad worked at Garston Docks until he retired in 1985. Although he enjoyed working as part of the dock community, he was always looking forward to the day when he could return to working with his beloved horses. He had a very busy retirement, helping at a nearby riding school for young people with disabilities, driving a brougham for weddings, judging at horse shows, stewarding at the Royal Lancashire Show and most notably, working for Granada Studios as a hansom cab driver in the *Sherlock Holmes* television series. He passed away suddenly in February 2007. He rode down Garston village one last time, though, in a horse-drawn hearse, before his remains were interred in the Joy family grave at Garston parish church.